D0834638

Single

Understanding and Accepting the Reality of It All

by
William A. White

Warner Press, Inc.
Anderson, Indiana

Published by
Warner Press, Inc.
Anderson, Indiana

Arlo F. Newell, Editor in Chief
Dan Harman, Book Editor
Cover by Larry Lawson

Contents

Dedication

To Park Place Singles of Anderson, Indiana, without whose friendship, insight, and support this project would never have been started, let alone finished.

To Park Place Church of God of Anderson, Indiana, for their willingness to provide an open door for ministry with single adults to take place.

To Arlene Hall with deep gratitude to God for her investment in and dedication to ministry with single adults and for her constant encouragement to me.

To Arlo Newell, a dear friend.

Foreword

"Bill White has written a simple, honest, and practical guide to living the many experiences of singleness. His own journey through single againness as well as his speaking and teaching ministry to single adults has given him a keen edge of understanding the many struggles and triumphs of the single person.

This is a book that deals honestly with Single . . . The Reality rather than Single . . . The Fantasy! It is both a handbook for living and a guidebook for personal and group study. It is a positive help for all single adults."

Jim Smoke
Tempe, Arizona
1990

Preface

Thinking I might find a use for the following, I wrote it down and filed it away some time ago. It wasn't quoted so I don't know its origin.

Those who can, do.

Those who can't, teach.

Those who can't teach, teach others to teach.

Those who can't teach others to teach, write books.

That may be partially true for me, but as I reflect on some other reasons why this book came to be I can think of at least three.

The germ idea, I believe, came from my own experience (having become suddenly single after seventeen years of marriage) and from an observation of single adults from all over the United States. As I have been privileged to lead Creative Singles Workshops and Divorce Recovery Workshops across the country, the idea has been obvious to me that some single adults, whether suddenly single or never married, have a difficult time accepting their singleness as real and okay and realizing that as single adults they can indeed have a rewarding and full life. I wrote the book hoping that those who read it will find some help in how to make that process happen.

This book also came into being because of the encouragement and prodding of Dr.

James Massey and Dr. Arlo Newell, who from time to time continued to say to me in their own ways, "It's needed and you're one who can do it." I wrote the book because their confidence in me gave me some of the motivation needed to get the job done.

And last, I believe the reason I wrote this book is because I felt the whole experience worthy of my time and effort. If only one struggling single adult can find a kernel of hope or a morsel of encouragement to live his or her life to the fullest because of this book, then I feel the time and effort well spent.

I realize that at this time many books about and for single adults have been written. I have found many of them most helpful in my journey. But not one of those who have written has seen the scene from my perspective. They have their own histories and I have mine. They write out of their experience and I out of mine. So I bring to these pages (1) fifteen years of living as a single adult; (2) the wisdom of countless single adults who have shared their struggles in workshops I have lead across the country; (3) the influence of workshops and seminars on all facets of single living I have attended; and (4) a sincere desire to help single adults realize that wholeness, fulfillment, and joyous living can be theirs through a conscious and determined commitment to God and God's plan for their lives.

Introduction

C. S. Lewis said: "Think of me as a fellow-patient in the same hospital who, having been admitted a little earlier, could give some advice."

I trust that thought will pervade your reading as you proceed through these pages. Only realize that the advice is coming from not just one patient but from many since the book is a sharing of experience from the many, single adults I've encountered in my journey.

This book is only an introduction to the many facets of single adult life. I believe it will have fulfilled its purpose, however, if it is found to be objective in its approach and helpful in its effort to speak effectively to single adults. It must speak to those who want to make the most out of who they are, where they are, as they courageously deal with the issues and reality of *being single*. Hence, the book's underlying premise is that it's okay to be single. It does not suggest that one should give up on the possibility of a future marriage but, simply put, it means, if I'm not married, then I am single, and because that's reality, I intend to enjoy who I am and develop myself into the best I can be. My hope is that the book will provide some of the motivation and courage to live fully in the here and now. You need also to know that the book is written from a Christian perspective, a life-style that I believe is not only worthy of my best effort but one that I've found most rewarding here and now.

The book deals with thirteen issues facing single adults today. These are by no means the only issues, but I believe them to be most important. They rose to the top of the list of concerns because these issues came up again and again at workshops and seminars I have led throughout the country.

A brief summary of the book's content can be summed up as follows: The book examines some of the myths, advantages and disadvantages, and the dangers of being a single adult and explores some ideas about how to move toward a wholesome acceptance of the single adult life-style. A section of the book reviews our freedom as single adults and how it relates to our citizenship, choice, accountability, and God. The book goes on to support the idea that single adults can be whole persons as single adults and that that wholeness involves balance. It recognizes some of the hindrances that keep us from, and the helps that lead us to, experiencing a high self-esteem. It goes on to examine the many facets of loneliness and aloneness and provides a design for an action plan to deal with loneliness effectively. It looks at and suggests ways to put into practice some proven methods of developing and maintaining effective friendships. The book then surveys the purpose of dating and analyzes ways to meet people of the opposite sex and maintain healthy dating relationships. From there, a working definition of intimacy is considered and its relation to our sexuality and to celibacy. A working definition of the kind of intimacy we need today is also explored. It then takes a serious look at reasons relationships fail and ways to get out of a relationship that has gone sour. It considers answers to some important questions related to whether or not one is ready for a future marriage. The book continues by surveying the effects of being a single parent and provides some insight into how to deal with those effects It provides some encouragement not only to become aware of our spiritual side but to determine what will be required to nurture and develop it effectively.

If you find the book helpful, pass it on to others whom you know may benefit from its pages.

Leader's Guide

You may want to know that a Leader's Guide is available from Warner Press (Anderson, IN) under the same title. The guide provides material for a leader to use this text with a group (possibly a Sunday school class or weeknight study) for thirteen weeks in hour-long session periods. Purpose statements for each session are given and material needed as well as six to nine steps to follow to effectively accomplish each purpose. The book's division of thirteen chapters lends itself well to a quarter's study should someone want to use it as an adult elective. It can be ordered from Warner Press, 1200 E. 5th St., Anderson, IN. 46018.

Question: "Is singleness a problem to be solved or a mystery to be experienced?"
—Harold Ivan Smith

The Reality of Being Single

I heard Jim Smoke, long-time single's leader, tell this story sometime ago. I'm not sure it happened to him or someone else. A counselor was listening for the first time to a new patient. He hadn't had time to review any statistics about her and so simply met her and asked her to share why she wanted to talk to him. After ten minutes into the interview he stopped her because her statements were not tracking and asked, "Are you divorced?" to which she replied, "Oh no, I'm between marriages."

But, reality says if you're between marriages you are single, and for some single adults that's not an easy word for them to identify themselves with. It may be difficult for you at this time in your life, if you've just become suddenly single. But the sooner you are able to accept the reality of your single adult status, the quicker you can proceed with getting the most out of this fascinating yet challenging station in life. This chapter will look at some of the particulars of that adjustment and some ideas about ways to move toward positive acceptance.

Myths

Let's begin by examining some of the myths that have been perpetuated about the single adult life-style. If we were to use the media to judge what a single adult is, we could come to the conclusion that the majority of single adults are party animals, who live life making immature, selfish, and irresponsible choices. Hence, we could come to believe that to be single is wrong. That is one of the reasons some of our married friends nudge or urge us toward marriage. They see the fallacy of such a life and want something better for their friends. But, **(1) to believe that all singles are immature, selfish, and irresponsible is a myth.** We would have to agree that some are and live only for the moment's pleasure, but by far the majority of single adults I know are strugglers. They are committed to making the most out of the gift of life they have. They are determined to give themselves to something that will give this world a better tomorrow.

(2) Another myth is the belief that you won't be happy until you're married. The logic here is that marriage causes happiness and being single the opposite. It subtly suggests that single adults are failures and are probably very lonely. Not true. Some of you reading this have been in unhappy and lonely marriages. Marriage can't guarantee happiness. Whether you are married or single, you won't be happy until you are happy with yourself. That kind of happiness, I believe, comes from a personal relationship with God and a healthy, positive self-worth, which we will deal with in a later chapter.

(3) Another myth is that one requires a mate to provide a "family." While it is true we've come to accept the traditional family (one husband working, one wife at home, two children) as the norm or ideal, statistics tell us that only seven-percent of all the households in America fit the description. I'm not going to attempt to redefine the word *family* here, but given the present status of the different kinds of households that exist today, the word must be more inclusive. You may be aware of Carolyn Koon's story and her adoption of Tony. Carolyn has never married, and she adopted Tony when he was a small child. Is this relationship any less a family then the traditional one? Is a custodial parent of two children living in the same house any less a "family" because a former spouse is gone (either by death or divorce)? Is it true that to be a family, one must have children? If that isn't true, then are noncustodial parents and single adults who have never married any less a family? It seems to me that *family* is a much broader term and needs to be seen as such.

(4) Another myth is that for a single adult to determine the scope of his or her future without a spouse is difficult (maybe next to impossible). So, the best way to handle being a single adult is to put your life in a holding pattern until the right person comes along. In other words, put off buying that condo or making that investment, put off purchasing that appliance or taking that trip, put off taking that course or starting a new hobby, put off going to that single's group or getting involved in a support group. Single adults who live this way fail to realize that life is *now* as well as in the future. Some single adults, however, are taking charge and realizing that their futures are in their control as they utilize the present. They are living for today and not postponing their life until Prince Charming or Cinderella comes along.

(5) Another myth, particularly visible in the church, is that single adults have all the time in the world and energy to burn and therefore are always available for volunteer work. I guess this is one of the drawbacks of our freedom. People tend to think that because we don't have the kind of responsibilities married people do, we must have time on our hands. Not so. Building a positive Christian life-style takes time and hard work, whether married or single. Single parents have similar responsibilities of marrieds with children, only they are doing it alone, which sometimes makes the job overwhelming. Single adults are working hard on developing a future whether it will be with or without a spouse, which includes deciding on a career and building positive friendships.

Adults suddenly made single by death or divorce are working on dealing with transition and change and the hard work of quitting their marriages and moving on. All of this takes responsible living and quality time.

(6) Another myth is that the single life-style is a breeze. Nothing to it. Being single is no big deal. Not true, if for no other reason than that life worth living takes courage, whether one is married or single. It takes courage to discipline freedom to make it work for you instead of against you. It takes courage to deal constructively with loneliness and to develop a healthy self-worth. It takes courage to assume responsibility for choices and decisions that need to be made. It takes courage to develop effective listening skills and workable communication competence and put them into formative action in starting, nurturing, and maintaining positive, growing friendships.

If, for whatever reason, you've assumed any of these myths to be true for you, part of the journey toward acceptance of your single adult status will be to face them honestly and attempt to remove them from influencing your attitude. They are roadblocks to a healthy single adult life-style.

Comparisons

When we honestly look at the single adult life-style, what ascends to the top as some of the advantages and disadvantages? It could be that as we make some comparisons we may feel differently about it all.

First, a list of advantages. Add to the list any others you may think of:

Freedom and independence

Time for unparalleled self-exploration (getting to know the real you)

Time to develop and pursue a career as you wish

No more fighting (for some, because the former spouse is gone)

Provides you with privacy

Gives you the privilege to choose, make personal decisions

Allows you to take control (this can be scary, but help is available if needed)

Provides the excitement of forming and maintaining friendships you choose

Allows you to pursue any dream or goal single-mindedly

Others:

_____

_____

_____

Now, a list of disadvantages. Again add to the list any others you think of.

Loneliness

Closeness of intimacy missing

Constant social pressure to marry

Uncomfortableness around married people (can't seem to make close friends with them)

No one to help share the work (or sit and listen, enjoy the stars, bring the soup when you're sick)

Voice and presence of another missing (companionship)

No children or grandchildren (for some), hence missing the growth process

Heavy financial responsibilities to carry alone (for some)

Uneasiness caused by feeling that others see you as a loser, and so forth.

Others:

_____

_____

_____

If you've never compared these lists you might like to do so, and mentally weigh them in terms of how they affect you. Have you been more concerned about the disadvantages and missing some of the advantages? Another helpful list to make is the advantages and disadvantages of marriage. Then make further comparisons. If you find you have been too obsessed with the disadvantages, a change of attitude and opinion is always an option.

Dangers to Avoid

The reality of being single poses some dangers that can sap life rather than embrace it. In addition to **(1) putting your life in a holding pattern** (myth #4) you could **(2) see yourself as a loser,** which in turn may affect your seeing other singles as losers as well. You could **(3) get stuck blaming or being angry with your parents or a former spouse or both** and because of the dominance of these feelings have no room for positive feelings of joy, kindness, peace, and the like. You could **(4) let freedom ring without any accountability, and that can be devastating** to healthy growth. You could **(5) see marriage as the only way to wholeness** and miss out on the advantages of your season of singleness. You could **(6) refuse to accept the reality of your singleness** and never get on with the hard work of making the most out of your present state—that being to develop into a positive, healthy, Christian single adult. You could **(7) get stuck having single friends who despise their singleness** and by their constant complaining cause you to become sour about the single adult life-style.

All of these dangers are traps we can easily fall into. No one can avoid them but you. You must take control. No one can do it for you. If you feel you need some help, it's always a sign of strength to see someone you trust who can give you an objective opinion.

Journey Toward Acceptance

We've looked at some of the myths about single adult living, made some comparisons with the advantages and disadvantages of the life-style, and reviewed some of the traps single adults can fall into. Part of moving toward accepting the reality of your singleness is coming to grips with the issues these raise for you (as has already been suggested).

Another step toward acceptance involves changing your attitude. For those suddenly made single the normal feeling in the beginning of the transition is to feel angry and rebellious (mad at the former spouse, at God, and the world). To feel sorrow over the loss of a relationship is normal. To feel isolated and lonely is normal. To feel rejected or like a failure is normal. If you've never been married, it's normal to feel that something must be wrong (particularly if a parent or friend keeps making remarks like "What's a nice person like you doing not married?"). *However*, even though these feelings exist, they are not normal if they continue to dominate your every waking hour. Even though you have become suddenly single or haven't as yet made it "from single file to center aisle" these feelings can and should eventually be replaced. In part it has to do with our knowing and accepting as fact that "I have worth." One of the major themes of the Bible is that God, through Jesus Christ, frees us to love ourselves for

9

who and what we are **because** God accepts us that way. In effect, God says to each of us, "Your marital status is not most important to me, it is your self-status that makes you important." God, who created us, says we have worth. God wants the best for each one of us. God accepts us fully, whether we're married or single. Regardless of where we are, God says, "It's okay to be you." God also says, "Let me help you make the most of who you, are where you are."

Even though the marital status most widely found in the Bible is that of marriage, the single life-style claims a prominent place in the life of the men and women of the Bible who made a difference in their worlds. The fact is well established that Jeremiah, Hosea, John the Baptist, Mary and Martha (probably Lazarus), and Paul were single. They all played important parts in God's unfolding plan. Jesus could be added to the list as well; however, some may discredit the importance of it because his singleness was not like ours in that he was both human and divine. Regardless, he made a profound contribution to our understanding of this issue when he responded to his disciples' question about the high demands of marriage (Matthew 19:1-12). In essence, he offered both marriage and the single life as proper and demanding options. In other words, he said, It's okay to be married and it's okay to be single.

Now, you may decide that you need to be

married. The wish is worthy. We don't need to discredit it by denying it. However, to move from seeing it as a **need** to seeing it as a **want** might help. Because you are single, you could move toward affirming (and even celebrating) who you are, where you are. You could work hard at developing yourself into the most positive single adult possible and then take that self into new relationships as healthy and whole. You may want to marry. Realizing it as a want instead of a need takes some of the pressure off and can allow more concerted effort to being devoted to being the best possible you.

Because God can (and is more than willing to) give us worth, we can see life as a gift. Whether we are married or single, we can make some choices that can help us make the most out of who we are, where we are. It is possible for single adults to be satisfied enough with their status to be able to say with assured confidence: It's okay to be single. I trust if that's not part of your affirmation, it soon will be, because if you're single now, *that's reality*.

"The basic test of freedom is perhaps less in what we are free to do then in what we are free not to do."*

—Eric Hoffer

The Reality of Freedom

In any list of pluses related to the single adult life-style, freedom, or some form of it, seems to float to the top. Some of the reasons seems to be (as one would compare single life with married life, for example) (1) I don't have to account for myself to a spouse; (2) I don't need to compromise my plans; (3) I can develop my individuality and create the quality of my own existence; (4) I can go wherever I want to go in a moment's notice; (5) I can decide on my own purpose for living.

For some single adults, this freedom has meant doing whatever they want, wherever they want, with whomever they want. As a result they have become slaves of their passions and are usually selfish people, which has in part given some married adults the idea that single adults are irresponsible, immature, sex-craving swingers. Many single adults, however, use their freedom to become responsible citizens by both civic and religious choices that have the betterment of the whole in mind.

I remember reading in a Reader's Digest a quote by Martin Buxbaum who defined freedom as "being able to do what you please without considering anyone except your wife (if you have one), the police, your boss, your life insurance company, your doctor, your airline, federal and state authorities, and your neighbors." I'm sure there are those who feel this to be true for them. However, according to the dictionary, to be free means to be released, liberated, delivered from whatever binds or suppresses. The stoic idea of freedom is that the free person is always master of himself or herself and never the slave of circumstances.

Freedom and Citizenship

Living in America we possess the benefits of a republic, under constitutional government, which grants us certain freedoms. We have been granted the freedom of speech, freedom of religion, freedom of the press, and freedom of assembly, to name a few. We can, if we so choose, have a voice in how we are to be governed. That voice is terribly weak during election time, however, since so few bother to vote.

Because of our collective freedoms, many have chosen values that have endeared themselves to meaningful living. Is not freedom at the root of honesty, courage, fairness, generosity, religious conviction, and love? Our freedom has also allowed the choice of just the opposite as well. But we know the difference and, I believe, prefer the former.

There is also a connection here between my freedom and my granting you yours. Clarence Darrow said, "You can protect your liberties only by protecting the other man's freedom. You can be free only if I am free."

Freedom and Choice

I remember reading a true story about a woman who had been completely paralyzed at age 31. Naturally, she was overwhelmed with the feeling of being imprisoned in a body that would not allow her to run, dance, or carry her children. But in response to her situation, one day she realized she still had the freedom to make choices. She could smile or weep, be mad at God or ask for strength, be a role model for her children or wither and die. She chose to replace one freedom with another and transcended her physical limitations by expanding her mental and spiritual qualities. She gave the world a smile with God's help and became a model for not only her children but the world as well.

Some single adults feel imprisoned by their singleness. They have accepted the philosophy of those who have defined the single life-style as a negative, a way of life that makes one half a person with a hopeless and lonely existence. However, they also have the freedom of choice. They can choose to make their life, whether single or married, a positive whole. They can choose to examine the depths of loneliness and learn how to deal with it in positive, creative ways (see chapter 6). They can choose to accept their freedom of choice and use it to enhance the quality of their life, in turn enhancing the lives of others in positive ways. It's their choice.

Freedom and Accountability

Let's begin with a claim: The lack of accountability can negatively effect single adults and the development of their fullest potential.

Do you agree?

To be accountable means that one is liable, responsible, tied to, answerable to someone else. My grounds for the claim are based more on personal testimony and observation than on statistical data. As I reflect on my own growth as a single adult and observe and talk to other single adults as I travel across the country, I have noticed single adults who have no purpose and seem to be living stagnant, unproductive lives. They are making little or no contribution to life and yet seem very capable of doing so. I'm aware that many reasons could account for this. I'm wondering, however, if freedom may be connected. Because I can go where I want, when I want, with whom I want and because I don't have to ask anyone's permission, I could develop a selfish life-style. A helpful book picturing this life-style in clear and concise terms is Christopher Lasch's, *The Culture of Narcissism*.

To me the experience of life seems to suggest a correlation between accountability and personal growth. For someone other than myself to know of my goals and progress seems to help me achieve them.

All of this poses more questions than answers. For example: Am I free if I'm accountable? What is my fullest potential as a human being? Does mine differ from yours? How? What are the connections between accountability and (1) commitment, (2) God, (3) my body, (4) failure, (5) discipline, (6) deceit, (7) goal setting, (8) caring, (9) self-worth? If accountability is connected, how can we build it into our lives? What kind would be good for me?

Naturally, some of these questions are difficult if not impossible to answer—In part because this whole issue may be founded on an erroneous claim. But for me and from my limited observation, I feel there is a correlation between accountability and personal growth. Maybe it has to do with my freedom to choose some significant others to be involved in my growth in all areas of my life. I've been fortunate to have involved people in my growth—physically, intellectually, emotionally, and spiritually. I guess in part their involvement came to be because I believed I needed help to make the most out of my life. I believe that the more I'm responsible and answerable to God, others, and myself, the better able I am to make a little more sense out of the chaos that's part of our world.

Freedom in Christ

The *Interpreter's Bible* gives a religious definition of freedom as a "state of those who are not slaves; the quality of personal and social life, here and hereafter, which is the given possession of those whom Christ has set free from human bondage."

The New Testament teaches us that we are in bondage to sin. It's universal. Romans 3:23 says "all have sinned and fall short of the glory of God." In Old Testament times followers of God found themselves in bondage to the Law (Ten Commandments and the like), which was incapable of enabling them to achieve righteousness. Many adhered to it believing it could bring freedom from sin, but it didn't. Hence, we were in bondage to death and decay, *until*, Jesus Christ. God in Christ became a human being, assumed flesh, took the form of a slave, yet, remaining sinless, "condemned sin in the flesh" (Romans 8:3), and brought human nature to its divine destiny. For "God raised [Jesus] up, having loosed the pangs of death, because it was not possible for him to be held by it" (Acts 2:24, RVS). As we believe and trust in this "liberator," Jesus Christ, we can be free of being captive to sin (2 Corinthians 5:21), the law (Galatians 5:5, 18), and death (Romans 6:23).

But, Christian freedom is not simply freedom *from*, and definitely not license *to* do as you please. Christian freedom frees us *to* be a "slave" (in its positive sense, servant) of God *to* love others. "You were called to freedom, brethren; only do not use your freedom as an opportunity for the flesh, but through love be servants of one another. For the whole law is fulfilled in one word, 'You shall love your neighbor as yourself' " (Galatians 5:13-14, RSV).

Being crucified with Christ and raised to a new life in him (Romans 6:3-4), we are no longer slaves to the flesh, no longer alien from God, no longer exempt from God's service. We have now become sons and daughters, desiring to do our Father's will and abide in his house forever.

From Paul's letter to the Galatians we can catalog what free in Christ means. We are free through Jesus Christ to (1) inherit God's promises; (2) live according to the Spirit; (3) express the fruits of the Spirit; (4) serve one another in love; (5) restore anyone trapped in sin; (6) do good to those who believe; (7) become a new creation.

What have we said? As a citizen of the United States of America I am free from oppression to enjoy the benefits of what that freedom has brought to me. I can be thankful and trust I won't take it all for granted. Part of that freedom involves me in my freedom to choose. I can choose how I'm going to respond to life and its challenges. My freedom of choice frees me *from* being controlled by circumstances *to* an acceptance of life, even though it may not be to my liking at times. My freedom is enhanced when I see it not as a license to do as I please with whomever I please whenever I please, but as a gift that helps me grow as I allow myself to be accountable to others, and particularly to God through Jesus Christ. My freedom as a citizen also gives me the opportunity to develop my spiritual side by telling me I can worship and serve the god of my choice. Many choose "a lesser god" (like materialism, power, sex, or popularity). The New Testament is clear, I believe. In Jesus Christ I can be free *from* being captive to sin and death *to* be a servant of the God of love. It's as simple and profound as that.

"Wholeness is a healthy embracing of all parts of life."*
—Ann Kiemel Anderson

Chapter 3

The Reality of Wholeness

Can anyone in the whole wide world stop and say, "Now, I know beyond any shadow of doubt that I'm a whole person?" Are some people more whole than others? Are married people more whole than single people? What is wholeness anyway? Can I really have it? Do I want it? How much, if anything, does it cost?

In this chapter we will attempt an answer to these and similar questions. Our purpose will be to discover the meaning of wholeness and how it affects us as single adults.

Sometime ago I saw an ad in a magazine advertising a unique opportunity offered by a university. The ad pictured a golfball seemingly rolling into a hole. Being a golfer I saw the golfball first and then the caption: "We're excited about our *whole* in one." Having had two (2) holes-in-one in 1986 (true), I read on. The ad described an assurance that Azusa Pacific University in California was about the job of educating the "whole" person through its "whole in one" concept of Christian education. What was meant was that the concept promoted helping students discover their physical, intellectual, spiritual, emotional, and social potential. Neat idea and I'm sure they work hard at making the concept a reality.

The ad, in part, gives us a working definition of wholeness. It suggests we are multidimensional human beings (whether married or single). We are people with many parts or selves. Therefore, wholeness is related to wholeness of the parts. Wholeness deals with the inner life and workings of human beings. It suggests that we are whole as one but divided into individual parts (such as physical), each of which is also a whole needing special attention.

In an informative book titled *Struggling for Wholeness,* (Nashville, TN: Thomas Nelson, 1986) Ann Kiemel Anderson and her twin sister Jan Kiemel Ream provide some insight into this often perplexing subject. They define wholeness as a "healthy embracing of all parts of life." They mean the good and the bad, the joy and the sorrow, the gains and the losses, the successes and the failures. They suggest wholeness has to do with the ability to integrate all those parts into some kind of healthy outlook, so that inside there is a sense of joy, peace, and freedom.

At a workshop I was leading on this subject, someone defined wholeness as a "process of growing in grace and peace with God, others, and myself." I like that. It suggests a

24

state of becoming. I'm on the way. I know I'll never be completely whole. I believe my wholeness is in the journey, not in the completion of a whole person.

If wholeness then is a process toward wholeness of the parts, then wholeness seems to me also to involve balance. If I believe I'm a multidimensional being, a composite being as the ad suggests, then as much as is possible I need to give equal attention to all the parts. As I do, the balance achieved affects my total sense of wholeness in positive ways. However, I must realize that I do this balancing act by myself. Other people may be involved in influencing me, but in the end I am the one who must take the initiative. I'm the one who, in the end, must make the choices and the decisions. I'm the one who must set and work toward completing the goals. In this sense, marriage doesn't make me a whole person. In fact, this is one area in which single people and married people are on common ground. Whether married or single, the quest for balance is mine to make as an individual. Some facets of married life help me just as some facets of the single life also help.

Physically Whole

We seem to be in a fitness craze today. Sales are up in all areas related to aerobics, running, biking, and the like. Memberships to the YWCA and YMCA are up. Parks and streets are full of joggers, all of which suggests that people are interested in good health and long life. One person who has had a tremendous influence on this whole area is Dr. Kenneth Cooper of Dallas, Texas. He claims, from research and experience, that it is easier to maintain good health through proper exercise, diet, and emotional balance than it is to regain it once it is lost. He has attempted to prove that to us in eight books that have sold over seventeen million copies and that are now in thirty-nine different languages including Braille.

So, what does becoming physically whole mean? In part, at least, it means I strive to maintain a state of health and fitness appropriate to my body functions. It means I do what's necessary to learn about and participate in following good nutrition. It means I'm constantly increasing my level of understanding of how my body functions and how best to maintain it. In other words, it means I will set my sights on nothing less than an effective, personal health management course, which should include exercise, nutritious food, and effective stress management.

One way to start the course is to ask and answer some important questions: (1) What have I done lately to improve my health? (2) When was the last time I had a thorough physical examination and blood test? (3) What have I done lately to reduce my resting heart rate (which when reduced could extend my longevity)? (4) What could I do about my diet and my attitude toward food? (5) Have I had a stress test lately? (6) What should I know about cholesterol, HDL, LDL, and triglycerides?

Mentally Whole

An ad on television concludes: "A mind is a terrible thing to waste." How true it is, and too often we fill our minds with such trivia (could be the reason why the game is so popular). We make an assumption that after a hard day's work we need a little rest and relaxation. We do, but for some that means the TV goes on as soon as we step in the door and it stays on whether we're watching it or not. But eventually we do watch it and what we see fills our minds. Stop for a moment and take an inventory. Think back over the past week. How many hours per day did you watch it? What did you watch? We fall so easily into the entertainment trap, don't we? Two, three, or four hours can go by so quickly. Please don't misunderstand me, I'm not downing TV. We need to laugh. We also need to check what are we laughing at. There are some excellent, informative programs on TV that can help us better deal with life and the issues we face. I believe, however, that those programs take a back-seat to the regular fair of sitcoms, soaps, and crime that is available day and night.

Some of the marks, I believe, of a person becoming whole mentally (intellectually) include the following: a constant openness to new ideas and the wisdom of others; a passion to learn; an eagerness to stretch the imagination; a deep desire to "dream the impossible dream." What a magnificent intellect God has given us. We need to keep Paul's admonition to the Philippians in our minds constantly: "Whatever is true, whatever is noble, whatever is right, whatever is pure, whatever is lovely, whatever is admirable—if anything is excellent or praiseworthy—*think* about such things" (Philippians 4:8 emphasis added).

Spiritually Whole

I remember attending a seminar led by Jim Smoke on spiritual growth. I was fascinated by an answer he shared with us to the question: What is a right relationship with God? His response: It begins when one has heard the Good News that God proclaims to us in Jesus Christ, "I love you unconditionally, I have already given myself to you totally (in Jesus Christ), and now all that I ask is that you begin to respond to my love and commitment to you by giving to me all of yourself that you are able to give."

That to me suggests a way to spiritual wholeness. Receiving Jesus Christ opens the door for a relationship with God to begin. It is a progressive event that involves commitment, dedication, and loyalty all along the way. As I begin to receive God's love into my life, that love begins to express itself through

28

me to others. As I let that work its way through my attitudes, I am becoming whole spiritually.

I believe God truly wants us to love God and enjoy God forever. That seems to me to be at the heart of spiritual wholeness. Our calling is to reflect God's character, love, and image to those around us. But because we are human we are prone to reflect our own image, which often translates into sin and disobedience. However, Jesus Christ came into the world to answer our problem. He didn't come to set us free from our body or remove us from this world but to deal with the problem of sin here and now. He came to restore us to a right relationship with God.

Our calling then, to put it another way, is to trust in Jesus Christ and be restored to the image of God. In the very act of trusting and believing comes wholeness, not in the sense of completeness but in the sense that God's love has started and continues to grow and flourish in and through us. God's image works as a leaven both within us and in our relationships. The Greek word for *complete* is "teleios" and suggests that a complete person, biblically speaking, is one who is moving forward in all facets of her or his inner life. A "complete person" is one who lacks nothing in the sense that he or she has believed that God has all the bases covered. In other words, although we know we haven't arrived, God is always available to supply whatever we need to keep us moving forward.

We're called to be like God (Ephesians 4:24). Our calling then to spiritual wholeness is not to deface ourselves (be someone we're not, replace our personality). Nor is it to escape from the world. Jesus prayed for God's protection for us *in* the world (John 17:13-19). It is, however, to be in obedience to Jesus Christ, the true image of God, which restores us to that image, that likeness, and begin to reflect God's love and character to those around us. Spiritual wholeness comes as God's image and character become part of who we are. Our love for God and our desire to be like God, affect all that we do, because our spiritual growth and wholeness is at the very core of who we are, created from the beginning in God's image. This will be developed further in chapter 13.

Emotionally Whole

Understanding our feelings is not easy. But the challenge of emotional wholeness is just that. Alex Keaton of the sitcom *Family Ties* was talking during one episode with one of his girlfriends about feelings, and she accused him of not knowing what his were. In his esteemed way of responding he said, "Okay, okay. I'm going to the library and read all the books on how to identify my feelings and when I find out what my feelings are I'm going to memorize them."

Sometimes feelings are evasive to us. They can be identified and experienced, however, but there's no need to memorize them, mainly because they keep changing. They are powerful forces within the human mind and body. They come and go but as they do, they affect our behavior. They change in intensity (from high to low degrees of influence) and they change in emphasis (one dominates, then subsides as another takes over). They are amoral (neither good nor bad). As they affect our actions, however, our actions do have moral consequences. The challenge of emotional wholeness has to do with learning how to accept ourselves as okay with all of our feelings, both what we deem to be good and bad. The following is a partial list of some of these feelings: adoration, affection, anger, boredom, depression, fatigue, fear, guilt, joy, self-pity, loneliness, reflection, resentment, stress, and worry. These are feelings that come and go. Emotional wholeness comes about as we continually decide, day by day, that it is okay to be who we are, with all of our feelings.

I'm not suggesting that we find wholeness by freeing our emotions from restraint and inhibition, in other words, letting them take us wherever to do whatever. What I am suggesting is that we simply learn how to accept ourselves. Self-acceptance involves giving priority time to developing a healthy, positive self-worth. I can do that and so can you. In part I can do it by eliminating those patterns in my life that hinder me from feeling a sense of confidence and satisfaction in myself (behaviors like put-downs, comparisons, negative self-talk, hanging on to the past). On the positive side, I can enhance my self-worth by building on my strengths, helping others feel good about who they are, believing the Bible when it tells me I am of tremendous worth to God, and the like. This will be explored in depth in the next two chapters.

Socially Whole

I'm sitting in the Indianapolis airport writing this and watching people meeting their friends and relatives coming off the plane I'm about to board for St. Louis. People are fascinating to watch. In this grouping, women, by far, outnumber the men in being at ease with hugging and showing emotions (tears, joy, a smiling welcome). Men, either showing some embarrassment over public displays of affection or obviously pulling back to continue or regain their space, are wanting to move, to walk, to get to the baggage area. Interesting, because I thought we had turned a corner in this area. I thought men in general, whether married or single, were coming to realize that the role of showing no emotion was being replaced with more tenderness and caring. The conclusion was obvious from this limited sample that most of these men still had a long way to go.

Now I realize that this is only one opinion and observation. There are those I'm sure who see male and female roles in a different light. I'm sure there are reasons why some are hesitant in their ability to show emotion. Shyness, inadequate communication skills, inappropriate parental and peer models, and the like all have their influence on how we relate to one another.

What we mean by social wholeness has to do with coming to some degree of comfortableness in developing and maintaining healthy relationships. This necessitates learning and using effective communication skills (listening and confronting). If those I've learned aren't effective, I can unlearn those that hinder and replace them with those that work. I'm moving toward wholeness in this area when I realize that relating to others should be a priority in my life, because other people can provide a perspective on what being a healthy, effective human being means. In relationships, I can make some comparisons and contrasts that can go a long way in helping me get the most out of my short existence here on earth.

Conclusion

I trust that you've been impressed with the idea from this chapter that wholeness involves wholeness of the parts. It involves balance between the parts as well. If I believe I'm a composite being, then I need to give myself to the tasks that develop equally the wholeness of parts. I can't neglect my physical wholeness by spending all my time and energy on spiritual wholeness and vice versa—and on through the list.

You and I are significant as single adults. We can be whole, where we are, with who we are. It's a matter of outlook, balance, growth, and commitment. I made the first hole-in-one in Florida, the other, in Indiana. But I've learned that I can be "whole as one" whether I'm in Florida, Indiana, or wherever. If I could give you a gift, I would give you the gift of courage and enthusiasm to engage yourself in the journey. We don't have to consider ourselves half instead of whole because we're not married. If I'm depending on marriage to make me whole, I'm missing the mark. In a subtle way the song "With You I'm Born Again" by Shire and Conners suggests this. Again, I trust you don't misunderstand me here. I'm not down on marriage. I believe it to be a very worthwhile partnership, something to look forward to. But I am up on knowing that I can be whole as one, and take a whole person into my future with or without someone on a permanent basis.

"No one can make you feel inferior
without your consent."
—Eleanor Roosevelt

Chapter 4

The Reality of Too Little
Self-Esteem   Part I

Sometimes we feel like the guy who got up one morning and looked in the bathroom mirror only to see a dark cloud with the words, "Please stand by—we have temporarily lost your image." Or like the gal who ran into a mall and went to the information booth and asked: "Who am I and where am I going?"

All of this confusion is rooted in how we feel about who we are, and how we feel about ourselves is connected to our self-esteem. Someone has defined self-esteem as "a confidence and satisfaction in oneself." It's self-respect and self-worth. It's one's good opinion of oneself, an appropriate regard for one's own standing. It's that within us that tells us it's okay to be who we are. The definition suggests that it's always a positive. But experience tells us that our confidence and satisfaction in ourselves has degrees connected to it. Sometimes it's up and at other times it's in the pits. When our self-esteem is up or high, we're able to share ourselves with others, make positive comments about ourselves, give sincere compliments, and laugh at ourselves. When it's low, we put ourselves and others down, bully others, start rumors about others, tell lies, and brag about accomplishments.

So, if this vacillation is taking place in our lives, something is causing it. What are the influencers? Do some life events prevent us from feeling a sense of confidence in who we are? Do others help build it up? If so, what are they? In this chapter we will attempt to look at some of the hindrances and in the next we'll identify some of the helps.

Hindrances

Put-downs

Put-downs happen in at least two ways. We can and do put ourselves down. We are also put down by others, sometimes intentionally and sometimes unintentionally.

Every once in a while I catch myself calling myself stupid. I know I'm not, but somewhere in my past I must have learned that's what you do when something you do doesn't come out the way you intended. This has also been called negative self-talk. Other phrases include these: I'm no good at anything; I wish I weren't so short (tall, fat, skinny); I just hate myself. All of these subtly suggest that I'm not worthy to be alive. All this could lead to the poor-little-me pity party. It's the feeling that everybody is against us, even God. Pity parties bring nothing but gloom and doom, which negatively affect our feelings of confidence and satisfaction in ourselves.

The other put-downs come from outside of ourselves. They come from family, friends, acquaintances, and enemies. They come from neighbors and associates at work and from people at church, through words, phrases, and gestures. They come through gossip and criticism. They come in phrases like, "You're so ugly you have to sneak up on a mirror," or "If brains were dynamite, you wouldn't have enough to blow your nose." They are couched in words like, Can't you ever do anything right? You'll never make it in today's world. What's a nice girl (guy) like you doing not married? What a nice dress. Did you get it at the Salvation Army? These are intentional put-downs. There are also unintentional put-downs. These happen when the person didn't mean to put you down, but you felt the pain of it anyway. A good example is found in Sidney Simon's *I Am Lovable and Capable* (Niles, IL: Argus Communications, 1973). The main character in the book is Randy. He decides to call a girl for a date. He's a little apprehensive about it, so he writes out what he thinks the conversation will be.

Me: Hello, Lisa, this is Randy.

Lisa: Oh hi, Randy, how are you?

Me: I'm fine. I just wanted to know what you're doing Saturday night.

Lisa: Nothing so far.
Me: Well, would you like to go the movies with me?
Lisa: Oh Randy, I'd love to.

Now, he's ready. He dials the number. She says "Hello."

He says "Hello, Lisa, this is Randy."

She says, "Randy who?" and Randy hangs up the phone, dejected and unintentionally put down.

The major problem with put-downs is that we tend to believe them. Although at the time we may be able to shrug off the sting, subconsciously we begin to believe what others may say about us. Naturally, if I believe I'm no good at whatever, I probably will not be good at it.

You may have heard about the proven experiment with the walleye pike. If you put a walleye into an aquarium with some minnows, the walleye will do what is quite natural and eat them. If, however, you put a clear glass partition in the middle of the aquarium, separating the walleye from the minnows, it will again do what's natural. It will see the minnows, swim toward them, hit the glass, and fall back. Still hungry, it will do it again. After a few attempts, the walleye will hit the glass with less intensity and eventually give up the quest. It "learns" that it can't have it's natural food. The amazing fact about this, however, is that when the glass is removed, the minnows swim right under the walleye's mouth and it won't eat them because it has "learned" that they must not be food anymore.

Put-downs are like that. Someone insinuates we can't do a certain task, react a certain way, or be a certain kind of person, or whatever. We hit the glass and eventually give up. The result of all this hinders our sense of confidence and satisfaction in ourselves.

Comparisons

Either consciously or subconsciously we compare ourselves with others. When we do we can run into difficulty. There is nothing wrong with being good looking (which is relative) or smart or creative or being an achiever with a good job and substantial income. The problem is that when I compare myself with someone else's looks, brains, artistic or athletic ability, job, or income and feel I need to be like them to be somebody and know I'm not, then I could feel cheated and that something must be wrong with me. When that happens, I feel I've lost my sense of confidence and satisfaction in myself. I need to remember that someone will always look better, have a higher IQ, more ability, and a better job and higher income than I do. I need to remind myself constantly, however, that no one can do what God intends for me to do. I am God's unrepeatable miracle, unique in every way. No one can be a good me, except me. I don't need to compare myself with anyone. "I was born an original. I don't need to die a copy," says motivational consultant Dave Grant.

Paul gave the Galatians some advice worthy of our consideration. The following is a personal paraphrase of Galatians 6:4: "All of us should test our own actions. Then we can take pride in ourselves, without comparing ourselves to somebody else." Otherwise, when we do and come up short, our sense of self-esteem is negatively affected.

Imaginary Illusions

The mind is a wonderful and marvelous part of creation. But for whatever reason, it can play tricks on us. With it we can make some of the most ridiculous assumptions about ourselves and others that can be made. I can, for example, come to the conclusion that I should be able to make everybody happy or that I should be loved by everybody or that I ought to be able to do everything well. I can, for example, come to believe that others should take care of me or at least be able to read my mind and know what I need. Above all, others shouldn't frustrate or irritate me. How absurd and unrealistic—and yet, when we ourselves or others don't measure up to some of these demands, we get angry and feel a bit of our confidence and satisfaction in ourselves drop into the low range.

Hanging on to the Past

"It's not like it was in the good ole days," we moan. "That's not the way it was done last time," we notice. "Christmas use to be such an exciting and eventful time," we remember. Some single adults live in their

42

memories and in so doing have nothing left to embrace the present. The past is past. We can learn from it. The future is out there. We can plan for it. What we have is the present. Living in your misty past, unwilling to quit your marriage (if that's what is needed), or refusing to make a necessary change leaves you in the middle of nowhere—and nowhere chips away at a high sense of confidence and satisfaction you could have about yourself.

Fears, Guilt, and Failure

These, along with rejection, self-pity, resentment, doubt (the kind that leaves you helpless), regrets, and others, all effect our self-worth and self-esteem negatively. Fear seems to immobilize us. We know what we want but fear stops us from taking any necessary action. If we attached any degree of self-improvement to what we want and, because of fear, don't accomplish it, we diminish our sense of confidence and satisfaction in ourselves to that degree. Guilt pulls our spirits down and failure causes us to retreat. Similar remarks could be made of the others in the list. It's true that some of them have some positive aspects to them, but they are all hindrances that negatively affect our sense of self-esteem.

In addition to looking at some possible ways to deal with some of these hindrances, the next chapter will focus on some steps we can take to build up our sense of confidence and satisfaction in ourselves.

"Jesus consistently lifted the worth of human life above the minimum levels to which the ancient world had reduced it. 'Of how much more value,' he said, 'is a [person] than a sheep.' He asserted that people were worth saving, that the individual member of society had inestimable value in God's sight."*
—Sherwood Eliot Wirt

Chapter 5

The Reality of Too Little Self-Esteem   Part II

In the last chapter we discussed some hinderances to feeling okay about who we are, hindrances that produce in us a low self-esteem. In this chapter we will consider a number of proven ways to build up our self-esteem, ways that can help us feel good about who we are.

The Helps

Eliminate the Negatives

Naturally, one of the obvious helps is to work at doing away with one or more of the hindrances, as they are identified. The library can be of tremendous help in providing information about any of the hindrances mentioned in the last chapter. You may be able to attend a conference or seminar on a particular interest. It's a known fact: as the hindrances are minimized, one's self-esteem begins to build.

God and Self-Esteem

What does the Bible say about our self-esteem? I believe we can safely assume from many passages, as well as the whole tone of the Bible, that God wants the best for us. That includes feeling a sense of confidence and satisfaction in who we are. That's God's desire, as I'm sure it is ours. But we live in a human world and interact with human beings. As a result we experience different reactions from other people. Some react with compliments and thanks others with judgment and rejection. When others don't accept us for who we are, we experience the feeling of a low sense of self-esteem. God still cares, still loves us, but we have to be realistic about our need for others to care for and love us, too. God won't stop others from hurting us, but God has promised to supply what we need to see it through. This comes to us through prayer, Bible study, and the work of the Holy Spirit in our lives.

Another way to look at it would be to consider a major theme that runs through the whole Bible: that being the "image of God." In Genesis 1:26-27 we read, "Then God said, 'Let us make [humans] in our image, in our likeness.' . . . So God created man in his own image . . . male and female he created them." Then in Colossians 1:15 we read, "[Jesus Christ] is the image of the invisible God, the firstborn over all creation." And last, in Romans 8:28-29 we read, "We know that in all things God works for the good of those who love him, who have been called according to his purpose. For those

God foreknew he also predestined to be conformed to the likeness of his Son."

All of these passages seem to relate to one another. They say to me that within every human being is the image of God. But the meaning is also clear that that stamp, that image, that likeness wasn't fully revealed to us until Jesus Christ, himself the image of God, came in the flesh to show us the true image of the Father. As a result I now know what that image is as I let Jesus Christ, the image of the invisible God, come into my life by faith. As I grow and conform to that image, I become like him as I live his life-style. What happens to my self-esteem in all this? By faith I come to realize that I am somebody, because God is at work in me as I conform to God's image in me.

For further study of the way God can be involved in increasing your self-esteem see David Seamands *Healing Grace* (Wheaton, IL: Victor Books, 1988), chapter ten entitled "Grace and Self-esteem."

Positive Addiction

I can also increase my self-esteem by becoming "positively addicted." Let me explain. Dr. William Glasser, through extensive research, has found that people who are positively addicted to something increase their sense of confidence in themselves. His book *Positive Addiction* (New York: Harper and Row, 1977) explains his research. Simply put, Dr. Glasser defines positive addiction as anything at all that a person chooses to do as long as it fulfills these six criteria:

(1) it is something noncompetitive that you choose and can devote approximately an hour to each day; (2) it is possible for you to do it easily and it doesn't take a great deal of mental effort to do it well; (3) you can do it alone (or, rarely, with others, but it must not require other participants); (4) you believe that it has some value (physical, mental, or spiritual) for you; (5) you believe that if you persist at it you will improve, but this is completely subjective—you need to be the only one who measures that improvement; and (6) you must be able to undertake this activity without criticizing yourself—if you can't accept yourself during this time, the activity will not be positively addictive.

According to surveys conducted across the country, people can and do become positively addicted to running or jogging (and any other of the physical sports, provided you don't feel the need to compete), meditating (could be prayer, Bible study and reading, and so on), daydreaming, knitting or crocheting, journal keeping (creative writing), playing a musical instrument, drawing, or the like.

What are some of the benefits? Many in the survey—by far the majority—reported that a sense of confidence and an increased mental strength they hadn't had before came back into their lives. Others describe weight loss or an ability to control their weight. Still others found the ability to give up bad habits or increase self-awareness and physical well-being.

Strengths and Weaknesses

I can increase my self-esteem by minimizing my limitations and maximizing my strengths. Sure, I know it's easy to say and hard to do, but it is possible. I've found that making two lists is helpful. One is a list of what I've identified as my weaknesses or limitations. The other a list of what I perceive (with others' help, if needed) to be my strengths. At first I found the weaknesses easy to list; but as I thought about it and even asked some friends who know me to help, I found I had some strengths that weren't readily noticeable to me but were to others.

As I review my list of weaknesses periodically, which I'm happy to say, has gotten somewhat smaller, I have come to a conclusion: **I can deal with my weaknesses as I accept responsibility for them**. I'm the one who "won't" (not can't) look dumb to others by sharing the way I feel about something. I'm the one who "won't" fight for what I believe because I've been raised to be passive. I'm the one who "won't" accept the fact that I can lose at anything and that I don't have to hate it with such passion that it causes explosive anger. I'm the one who stretches the truth a little to make me look better. I'm the one who "won't" assume responsibility for who I am. It's not something or someone else, it's me, regardless of the past. I've found that when I quit blaming others for who I am and deal as honestly as

49

I can with reality, I **can** make a difference.

I can maximize my strengths by acknowledging that I have some and by working at perfecting them. I can learn from my successes and come to believe that what God has given me is good. I can, for example, set goals related to my strengths. I can thank God daily for helping me be friendly and kind to others. I can list ways or places I can use my organizing ability and determine to work on specific areas. I can decide to use my zest for living in the most positive ways I can in helping others.

By minimizing weaknesses and maximizing strengths I can come to a better understanding of who I am and in the process come to feel that it's really okay to be me.

Building Others Up

I can also increase my self-esteem by building self-esteem in others. It seems to be some kind of reciprocal effect. The more I build self-esteem in others, the more I feel good about who I am. It may, in part, have to do with the fact that if I can make others feel good about who they are, they in turn may help others and in so doing begin to change the very fabric of life in our world. That makes me feel needed and gives me a feeling that I'm making a contribution with my life. So, my self-esteem is enhanced when I help people become aware that they are worthy. I contribute when I help people honor themselves as human beings who are uniquely created by God and who have worth and dignity regardless of physical appearance, intelligence, or material possession. The Bible suggests (1 Peter 3:3-4) that true self-esteem is related to the gentle and quiet spirit of being yourself, because what and who you are is beautiful. People around us need to hear that, and when it comes from our lips, it restores our self-esteem.

Positive Self-talk

I can increase my self-esteem by positive self-talk. One of the steps I took after my divorce was to attend a workshop led by Jim Smoke. I remember vividly a phrase Jim shared with the group. I find it most assuring and helpful. The phrase is, "I am an unrepeatable miracle of God, created in God's image, unique in every way." I have said that to myself a number of times and I've found as it sinks in, it does affect how I feel about myself. I am a worthwhile person. No one can do what I believe God wants me to do. I do have a purpose, and besides that, God has given his opinion of my value and it says I'm worth it (and I don't have to use L'oreal). Some other possible phrases might include these: "I am loved by God"; "I can, I' can, I can"; "If God is for me, who can be against me?"

We are so easily critical of ourselves. We are skillful at finding fault with ourselves. It's true, we are not perfect. We can remind ourselves of that. But internal criticism causes us to be guarded and uncertain of acceptance. On the other hand, learning to talk to ourselves in positive ways can and will help us feel that sense of confidence and satisfaction we need to face life courageously.

I think this chapter can be adequately summed up in Martha Graham's unique and challenging words which were shared with the participants of a workshop on self-esteem that I attended:

There is a vitality, a life force, a quickening, an energy that is translated through you into action. And because there is only one of you in all of time, this expression is unique, and if you block it, it will never exist through any other medium and be lost, and the world will not have it.

"We are born helpless. As soon as we are fully conscious we discover loneliness. We need others physically, emotionally, intellectually; we need them if we are to know anything, even ourselves."*

—C. S. Lewis

The Reality of Loneliness and Aloneness

Neil Diamond ends his once popular song "I Am, I Said" by saying that he had an emptiness deep inside of him that wouldn't let him go. He concludes he isn't a man who likes to swear, but that he never cared for the sound of being alone.

The suggestion here that loneliness is an emptiness that we hope to get rid of, and that sometimes it could make us mad enough to swear leaves us with the general feeling that loneliness is the pits. I think most of us would agree, and we could add a few other choice words or terms to further define it, like pain, restlessness, separateness, sadness, searching, frustration, the feeling that something is missing. All of this causes us or pushes us to try to escape, to find some relief, to move toward something, to connect with someone.

An examination of some of the myths that have been perpetuated about loneliness might be helpful in our discussion of this reality. It may also help us further define it.

Myths about Loneliness

Myth #1: Loneliness is something from which I can escape.

I think it's safe to say that everyone, young or old, man or woman, single or married, experiences loneliness. Maybe, in part, it's connected to our individual search for the meaning of our lives. We reach out to God and others and even deep inside ourselves for answers to who we really are and why we're here. When our search leaves us still searching, we experience loneliness. Of course, God understands us and wants to help us. God's wisdom and support are always available. But God doesn't promise to take all our loneliness away. God won't interfere with our freedom of choice either, which often leads us away from the kind of answers we seek and need. No one fully understands us, nor do we fully understand ourselves. When we feel desperate for understanding and don't get any, we experience loneliness. As much as we would like loneliness to go away, I believe it's part of being a human being. Hence, it will be with us throughout our life. So I don't need to escape from it. I need to learn to live with it.

Myth #2: Loneliness is for non-Christians.

The implication here is that Christians aren't lonely. Not true. Christians are as human as anyone else. If you've accepted that our loneliness is connected to our search for understanding, then it's plausible to me to believe that Christians can be lonely, too. There is a difference however. Christians do have the privilege to ask God for wisdom and support to deal with loneliness and learn from it.

Myth #3: Loneliness is something I can't choose.

Oh yes you can, and many do. Some single adults are so afraid of intimacy, that they settle for loneliness. Some don't desire to develop needed communication skills and as a result, consciously or unconsciously, choose loneliness.

Myth #4: Loneliness can be cured if I get married.

That is possible, but it is not a dead-sure guarantee. Many of you reading this have been in lonely marriages. Marriage can't assure one of effective companionship. Two people who want companionship can have it at the expense of giving quality time to build it.

Myth #5: Loneliness is impossible to experience in a crowd.

Many of us have felt the separateness at a ball game, on a bus, or at the mall. People per se cannot help my loneliness, but rather true companionship of dear and trusted friends.

Myth #6: Loneliness is a single's problem.

Not true. Singles are not the loneliest people in the whole wide world, simply because loneliness is a human concern. Some singles may think their loneliness is unique to them, but it is something that touches every human being. It is a human problem.

Myth #7: Loneliness is something I can get rid of.

Loneliness seems to be something that, despite times of relief, occurs again and again. It is continual. We experience the pain of loneliness more acutely at certain times (more about this later), but nevertheless we're going to feel its impact on our life throughout our life. Hence, we don't need to get rid of it but learn to face it head on because it has within it the power to help us grow and to become all we were meant to be.

Facing Loneliness Honestly

As mentioned earlier, we can come to realize at sometimes we are going to experience the pain of loneliness more acutely than at others. Knowing this won't take away the possible pain, but it could give us the chance to do something differently. Times when single adults feel loneliness more acutely than others might be on Friday or Saturday night, on birthdays or holidays, at weddings, when you have something to share and no one to share it with, when you feel misunderstood or when your self-esteem is low, when you have a decision to make or when you just don't have any energy. If you become aware of these times before they happen, plans could be made in advance that could soften the blow. If, for example, you know Christmas is coming, you could make some plans to begin a new way to celebrate the season. If you're totally zapped of energy, you could work on some quality rest. If Friday's coming and there's nothing to do, you could work on a hobby or put together a photo album or read that exciting novel you just heard about or spend some time in a Bible exploration study.

We can also face loneliness honestly by distinguishing the difference between loneliness and aloneness. In your mind they may be one and the same. To many single adults I meet across the country, they are not. By far, the majority of singles I know define aloneness with words and phrases like solitude, a time to reflect and meditate, something to plan for or look forward to, a time to recognize and explore relationships, and so on.

Paul Tillich, in his book *The Eternal Now*, makes the distinction with these words: "Our language has wisely sensed the two sides of being alone. It has created the word 'loneliness' to express the pain of being alone. And it has created the word 'solitude' to express the glory of being alone."

If we buy the slight but seemingly significant difference in these words, it just may be that in the acceptance of the difference lies part of our solution. Elizabeth O'Connor in her book *The New Community* says: "In an understanding of your aloneness lies your freedom. The work of silence is to open the door and let in the knowledge of your solitary journey, and in time to make friends with it, and let it instruct you." Call it mental gymnastics or whatever, but maybe if we can move our minds to think about the times we know we are going to be by ourselves as times for refreshment and reflection, then therein lies the possibility of gaining some strength to deal more intelligently with times of pain and emptiness. In other words, as I realize through reflection and meditation who I am and how I cope, the better equipped I might be to handle those times when I feel misunderstood and lonely.

I think this is justly illustrated in the following true story of Maria Jose Hobday. It seems one day when she was twelve years old, she was being extremely obnoxious. Finally, her father just couldn't take it anymore and told her to get a blanket, a book, and an apple and get in the car. She did, and her father drove her eight miles out of town to a canyon area. Then he told her to get out of the car and spend the day by herself, since she couldn't seem to get along with anyone else. He told her he'd be back to pick her up in the evening. She got out angry, frustrated, and defiant. She cried and threw her blanket, book, and apple over the canyon ledge. A couple of hours of pouting and dirt kicking later she got hungry. After a bit of a struggle, she retrieved the apple, sat down under a pinon tree, and began eating the apple. At that moment she became aware of a change of attitude. She began to "see" the beauty around her. She began to reflect on her earlier actions. She became more objective about her behavior. She got in touch with her feelings. She found herself wanting to be a better person. It was a prayerful time, a time of deep silence. She began feeling that she liked being alone, and she began to feel good about who she really was. By the time her father came, she felt restored. He didn't press her with questions; she gave no impressions. But they both knew that something was different. Her father had dumped her into solitude and had challenged her to grow. Before she got out of the car, she thanked him, and from then on, she learned to love times of solitude, of contemplation, of prayer. She concludes by saying, "This habit of seeking solitude has stayed with me all these years."

We can also face loneliness honestly by learning to enjoy our own company. What we're talking about here is learning to make friends with ourselves. When we're friends with ourselves, when we've filled our inner selves with kind thoughts about who we are, when we begin to learn to enjoy our own companionship, then we can also begin to be a good companion to others. We're not talking about a selfish, self-centered, narcissistic life-style. The life-style we want to suggest is that it is okay to be me. We do not have to lord it over anyone or put anyone else down or to constantly be asking, "What's in it for me?" but rather we come to accept who we are as we are, realizing the great gift of life we've been given and desiring to make the best of it.

In her book titled *Celebrate Yourself* Dorothy Briggs includes a chapter called "A Friend for You." In it she lists some statements you can review to determine whether or not you're learning to enjoy your own company. These are just indicators. If you can honestly agree with the statements (or answer yes) then probably you are making friends with yourself. If you find an area of concern, you can begin to make some possible changes. Here's a list of just a few.

1. Do you treat yourself as gently as you would a precious friend? If not, why not?

2. Are you being friendly to your body by giving it nutritious food, adequate sleep, exercise, and physical checkups? If not, why not?

3. Do you let the natural child in you play for the pure fun and enjoyment of the activity without the pressure to compete, achieve, or produce? If not, why not?

4. Do you practice staying in touch with all of your senses to savor the flavor of each moment in time? If not, why not?

5. Do you take time to indulge your creativity, curiosity, and spontaneity? Do you give yourself permission to venture into something new? If not, why not?

6. Do you give yourself periodic gifts (some that cost nothing) that are gentle kindnesses to you? If not, why not?

I remember a young Spanish girl in Illinois who, after hearing this last question, jumped up and said, "I know what that means." I asked her to explain. She said she got up one morning, looked in the mirror, and told herself, "I'm going to do something good for you today." She went to work. On the way home she stopped in an expensive department store and bought a diamond earrings and necklace set. When she got home she put them on and looked in the mirror. After a moment, she backed away and with her finger pointed at herself. "I'm not going to be so good to you for a while."

We can also face loneliness honestly by learning the art of giving ourselves to others. You may have heard about a widow named Bea Decker who founded a fellowship, still in existence today, known as THEOS (They Help Each Other Spiritually). The fellowship is for people newly widowed or divorced. It provides a time to be with other strugglers dealing with similar issues and concerns raised by death or divorce. Out of her intense loneliness has come a caring fellowship of people. She gave herself to other people's grief and many have found creative ways to handle their loss and transition.

If you need some guidance on how you can give yourself to others, ask your pastor or seriously look at the world around you.

Someone is in need of your smile, your talents, your experience, your gifts.

You can also face loneliness honestly by beginning a new activity. The possibilities are endless. What have you always wanted to do but for one reason or another have not been able to? Is it something to do with travel? Does it involve people? Do you need to go back to school? Could it involve your apartment, exercise, weight loss, a hobby, journal keeping (for more information on this one call the Dialogue House in New York, 1-800-221-5844), lessons, letter writing, investing, or what?

In the book *Pilgrim's Progress*, as Christian was crossing the river, his heart failed him because he was afraid. He began to sink in the cold, dark waters. But Hopeful, his companion, helped him to stand, calling out loudly, "Be of good cheer, my brother; I feel the bottom, and it is good." Then Christian recovered his faith and passed safely through the waters to the Celestial City.

Sometimes loneliness overtakes us and it becomes a morbid motivation of all we do. We feel as if we're in a rut, which is nothing more than a grave with the ends kicked out. But the good news is that we don't have to be afraid of loneliness. We don't have to worry about being overcome by it. Be of good cheer, we can find some ground on which to stand. We can stand on the realization there will be times when we will experience the pain of loneliness more acutely then at other times, and knowing that can help us make plans to better handle those times. We can stand on the slight but significant difference between loneliness and aloneness. We can stand on the truth that we can learn to enjoy our own company. We can stand on the belief that as we give ourselves to others and their needs, we find the emptiness of loneliness diminishing in direct proportion. We can stand on the fact that beginning new activities can stimulate our lives to the point that loneliness can be no more than an irritation.

"We take care of our health, we make our roof tight and clothing sufficient, but who provides wisely that we should not be wanting in the best property of all—friends?"
—Ralph Waldo Emerson

The Reality of Friendship

We must begin with an assumption. In the front of Leo Buscaglia's book *Loving Each Other* is this quote: "We are each of us angels with only one wing. And we can only fly embracing each other." The author of the quote is Luciano De Crescenzo. The assumption: We need each other. If I don't believe that, then developing any kind of meaningful friendship is next to impossible.

So, if your independence suggests to you that you don't need anybody or that life is meant to be lived by the philosophy, "I'll do it myself," then this chapter is not for you. On the other hand if you believe that sharing your dreams, goals, fears, thoughts, or ideas with someone is important to you or that you can learn from others and gain a sense of support and encouragement from them, then read on.

What Friends Can Do for Us

One of the first thoughts we might consider is what companionship can do for us. On a feeling level we know the warmth that can come to us when we feel respect and understanding. Friends can do that for us. Friends can and do give us strength to meet life's frustrations and failures. Friends can and often do provide a "mirror" for us to "see" ourselves as we really are, with all the strengths and weaknesses. Friends can also help us feel needed. Learning forgiveness is another advantage of friendship. At times one or the other must say "I'm sorry." Human beings just function that way. When it happens, both are enriched. Friends can also be there when you need someone. So, realizing the advantages of friendship should give us some incentive to learn what we need to learn and develop what we need to develop so that genuine, effective friendships become a part of our lives.

The Qualities of Friendship

We are all, I'm sure, aware of some of the qualities that are most conducive to an effective friendship and some of the qualities that are most destructive. One survey I saw listed the following as most conducive (in order of importance): communication (can be learned), honesty, acceptance, forgiveness, concern and consideration, understanding, affection, respect, sharing, and a sense of humor (this would be second or third on my list). Those characteristics most destructive would naturally be the opposite of all these and we could add egocentric behavior, lack of time, lack of trust, jealousy, apathy, and judgmental behavior.

These are impressive lists. However, I know what goes into a good friendship and what hinders one. I think you do to. Knowing about these qualities, however, doesn't guarantee you or me lasting friendships. So, what else is needed?

The Ingredients of Friendship

Let me suggest four possibilities that I believe could be helpful. Effective friendships develop when we (1) give priority time to them; (2) assume responsibility for creating and nurturing a sincere interest in others; (3) work hard at getting rid of fear, shyness, and a judgmental attitude; and (4) move toward unconditional love.

If, when I find myself friendless, I could take a pill and have instant friends, it would be great. But life just doesn't work that way, does it? Friendships, however, will happen when I am willing to give them top priority. What do I mean? It will happen when I am willing to take time, energy, and just plain hard work to develop them. I'm sure you're aware that few accomplishments of value take place automatically. On the other hand, some significant happenings take place when we recognize what is important to us and commit ourselves to its nurture and development. You probably wouldn't be reading this if you didn't think friendships were important to you. I guess you have to ask yourself, How important are they?

I believe anybody can have almost anything they want, if they want it badly enough. Some time ago I went through an extensive physical examination. It revealed a high cholesterol level. Solution: change my diet and start a consistent exercise program or take pills. I opted for the former. Today my cholesterol level is under control. I took up jogging and changed my diet. There were (still are) times when I don't feel like running or eating health food but I'm committed to better health. I want it, badly. So I work at it. Friendships are as important to our social and emotional health as low cholesterol is to our physical health. You and I can have effective friendships when we assign them the kind of priority needed to cultivate them. **How much time are you going to assign to them?**

Second, you and I must come to a satisfactory answer to this important question: How can I create and nurture a sincere interest in others? The possibilities are many. For example, one way has to do with the art of asking effective questions. Questions can be used effectively to start and maintain revealing conversations. The kind of questions that are effective are questions that begin with who, what, when, where, why, and how. The most ineffective questions are those that can be answered with a yes or no. They kill a conversation instead of moving it along. Questions that help start and maintain a conversation might be, Where did you go on vacation (or where are you going)? What's the most fascinating meal you've ever eaten? How do you handle criticism? Who is your favorite TV personality and why? When is it most difficult for you to be alone?

Another way to create and nurture a sincere interest in others is by learning some basic listening skills. This is *not* difficult. If I've learned to listen ineffectively, I can unlearn what isn't working and relearn what will. What works can be illustrated by some self-examination. Think for a moment about the last time you felt someone really listened to you. What did they do? If you felt listened to, you probably noticed some of the following. The person looked at you, didn't interrupt you, didn't say what he or she thought before you were through, didn't argue or criticize you, and listened to your feelings as well as your words. Other listening skills can be used: standing near enough to want to hear, being genuinely interested in what was being said, nodding in response to what was being said, repeating something for clarification. These could become our guidelines. We know how it feels to be listened to, and so to create and nurture a sincere interest in others we need to learn these simple techniques. They can make a difference. **When will you start genuinely listening and with whom?**

You and I can also enjoy effective friendships when we work hard at getting rid of three major hindrances: **fear, shyness, and a judgmental attitude**.

A number of fears are connected with friendships—the fear of rejection, of the unknown, of being taken advantage of, of not measuring up, the fear of being hurt, and the fear of exposure (if you really knew me with all my warts, you would be horrified). These are only a few. All of these get in the way of our developing healthy friendships. Some fears are so deep-seated that professional help is warranted. If you've tried to overcome one or more of these and haven't been successful, possibly counseling might be in order. Another possible approach would be to exercise faith in the **fact** (Romans 8:31) that God is for you, and because of that you can find some of the necessary courage you need to take some risks.

Philip Zimbardo, professor of social psychology at Stanford University, has written a most extensive study of shyness in his book *Shyness: What It Is and What to Do about It*. He defines shyness as a "shrinking from human contact, often because of a feeling of inferiority or fear of taking risks." Shyness makes it difficult for us to meet new people, make friends, or enjoy good experiences. It prevents us from speaking up and expressing our opinions and values. To be shy is to be afraid of people. In his book he suggests that shyness evolves out of the particular experiences we have in the home, in school, and with peers. So, we're not necessarily born shy. Dr. Zimbardo says that at the core is "an excessive concern for security." It has to do with an unwillingness to experiment with life. Shy people lose out "by letting other people and situations control their reactions." Can all this be corrected? Accord-

72

ing to Zimbardo, it can. He does suggest, however, that for some, because of the severity of their shyness, professional help may be in order. But for most of us (his estimate is that forty percent of all Americans consider themselves to be shy), we can learn some skills in approaching and relating to other people effectively. For example, shy people can concentrate on how to handle compliments and how to start a conversation and keep it going. They can move to imagining desired consequences, rather then fearful situations. As mentioned before, they can concentrate on making eye contact and assume the posture of an attentive listener. They can also stop saying negative remarks about themselves. They can think about correcting what is wrong and decide to take small risks (saying hello to three strangers, for example) and build from there.

Shyness limits our vision of how life is meant to be lived in relation to others. It's important to deal with it because if we don't relate well to others, we are the big losers. We are the ones without friendships.

A judgmental attitude puts up walls that make friendship difficult to climb over. Jesus was quite explicit about this. In one of his sermons he says, "Do not judge, or you too will be judged. For in the same way you judge others, you will be judged, and with the measure you use, it will be measured to you" (Matthew 7:1). This judging happens to us in subtle ways. For example, I remember reading about a psychiatrist who, after careful research, concluded that the **first four minutes** that strangers meet will determine if they become acquaintances, friends, mates, or remain strangers. Her contention was that this is true because we make quick and unrealistic judgments about another person, which are usually based on appearance. Because of our preconceived ideas about other people, we easily put them into categories. Just by what a person may be wearing or how they're wearing it, we surmise, maybe subconsciously, "Oh, I know his (her) type." But we don't. I'm not sure I wholeheartedly agree with the idea of the first four minutes. But I do agree that we put people in little cubbyholes before we've had a chance to hear what they have to say. We think we know all about them because of our keen, astute observation, and the consequence is that we miss many good opportunities to meet and enjoy some special people who may not agree with our idea of how one should dress or act.

Instead of pigeonholing people we need to learn how to put other people before ourselves. Paul's words are an appropriate example: "Do nothing out of selfish ambition or vain conceit, but in humility consider others better than yourselves" (Philippians 2:5). The opposite of judging is being kind, humble, gentle, and patient with others. This is the kind of person we want for a friend. This is the kind of friend we ought to be to others. **What is a realistic plan for you to start relating to others in kind ways?**

This leads us into the fourth area that can influence our developing effective friendships: moving toward unconditional love. To love someone unconditionally means we put no strings on our caring for that someone. Conditional love says, "I'll love if . . . , or because . . . , or when. . . ." Unconditional loves says "I'll love you anyway." Unconditional love lives by the principle of no return. It says, "It would be nice if you could return my love, but if you cannot, that's okay, because love is its own joy."

Granted this is easier said then done but I believe part of the answer to my being able to do it lies in learning the true meaning of Matthew 22:37-39. Jesus was asked by some Pharisees what the greatest commandment was. He replied, "'Love the Lord your God with all your heart and with all your soul and with all your mind.' This is the first and greatest commandment. And the second is like it: 'Love your neighbor as yourself.' " It is obvious to us, I'm sure, that the world doesn't live like this. If we take our cues from the movies and TV, we lose. But if we determine with God's help to live to the best of our ability and to love God and neighbor as much as we love ourselves, then we'll find ourselves bucking the norm but enhancing the possibility of effective friendships. I believe it. I trust you do, too. **How will you put unconditional love to work today?**

"Dating is a lot like a snowstorm. You have to put up with a lot of flakes."

—Anonymous

The Reality of Dating

If you're reading this chapter, I am assuming that the issue of dating is of concern to you now, or you assume it will be in the near future. If you are not dating now for whatever reason and this is not a concern right now, the section in the chapter on "Coping When Not Dating" might be of more interest to you.

In the book (it looks like a magazine) titled *Futile: The Magazine of Adult Dating* by Sara Parriott this definition of a date is found: "a social engagement between two members of the opposite sex that comprises (1) awkward greetings, (2) contrived conversation, (3) feeble attempts at levity, (4) a groping for mutual interests, (5) adolescent endeavors at intimacy, and (6) clumsy and inadequate good-byes."

Most of us can identify with that. For some, those particularly who are divorced or widowed and have gotten the courage to get back into the dating arena, the turf has changed. Mom and dad aren't around to check out the participants or check on the activities. Since you are an adult, you can date whom you want, when you want, go where you want, and do (or don't do) what you want. I don't think it would be contested to say that sexual issues have changed since the fifties and sixties. Sex without commitment seems now to be more the norm rather than the exception, and I guess TV and the movies help to promote it. It's not an easy place to be for someone who desires marriage and commitment as part of their approach to relationships (this will be explored more fully in Chapter 9).

The Purpose of a Date

I remember asking what the purpose of a date is at a single's seminar and one immediate response was a free meal. Well, in addition to that, isn't a date suppose to be just plain fun and a wonderful way to get out of the house or apartment? It's a way to attend a cultural event or enjoy a good meal. A date can provide a process of elimination (as you date you're bound to discover some traits or qualities you don't want in a future mate; hence you eliminate certain kinds of prospects). A date could be a preliminary to marriage (as you date, the opportunity is available to get to know someone rather well, which gives you some idea of whether or not you want to spend the rest of your life with this person).

Limits We Put on Ourselves

Some singles get stuck in this whole process by limiting themselves. For example, they worry about what others think of them if they date so and so. The If-I-date-Harry,-what-will-Mary-think-of-me kind of thing. A lot of singles also make quick decisions about a prospective date because they have prejudged them, and this is usually based on appearance. "Oh, I don't want to date him—he's too fat," or "I'll not ask her out because she's too old (or young)." On and on we could go: too tall or too short, too educated or not educated enough, too outgoing or too silent, too frugal or too frivolous. Naturally, like any other kind of limit, these get in the way. Because of them many have missed some beautiful people who could have provided some delightful experiences.

What Do You Notice First?

This absorption with appearance seems to be important to most singles. I remember seeing a survey that answered what men notice first about a woman and what women notice first about a man. According to the survey, men first notice a woman's body (not too surprising given our culture's preoccupation), then face, clothes, smile, eyes, hair (all in that order of importance). What women, on the other hand notice first about a man, according to the survey, is his clothes, then eyes, body, face, smile, and hair. Height and hands were at the bottom of both lists. Liz Trotta from CBS News, however, has said, "When I meet a man, I notice his manners. I think poor manners extends to more than etiquette. It also means not being insulting or a showoff or a phony. I don't notice his looks at first; the verdict on looks can't come until his personality emerges." Well, as you think about it, what do you notice first? Next time you meet someone, check yourself out. Is what you're noticing what you want to notice or do you need to make some changes?

What Do You Look For?

To push this a bit further we might then ask, What are you actually looking for in a person of the opposite sex? In other words, what are some of the characteristics you look for in the person with whom you might want to spend the rest of your life?

You may have heard about the fellow who constantly complained about the girls he was dating. They were either too silly, too frivolous, too argumentative, and on and on. One day he announced that he had found the girl of his dreams. She was perfect in every way. But when he broke the news, he lacked the joy that should have accompanied the culmination of his long search. His friend asked, "What's wrong? You found the perfect woman, didn't you?" "Yes," was the reply, "but she's looking for the perfect man."

As we all well know, there is no perfect man or woman, and some singles are beginning to realize it, too. Overheard at a single's seminar were these words: "I've had it with looking for Mr. Right. Now I'm looking for Mr. Pretty Good."

Well, what are the qualities or characteristics one looks for in a prospective mate? I've asked this at numerous workshops across the country and what seems to float to the top are the following. What men look for in a woman is: honesty, self-confidence, self-control, a Christian experience, intelligence, attractive features (relative term because what may attract one may not be attractive to someone else), femininity (the idea here is usually that they look for a woman who likes being a woman), health consciousness, and compatiblility. What women look for in a man is self-confidence, masculinity (not big muscles but one who enjoys being a man), a sense of humor, a Christian experience, thoughtfulness, honesty, and a zest for life (no couch potato). Naturally, there are others, and some of these may not fit your list, but these seem to be the most important. We also compiled a list of what women and men aren't looking for: a person who needs no one (totally self-sufficient), one who is wishy-washy about everything, the poor-me/woe-is-me type, the bore, and the person who is constantly wearing a mask, never being him or herself.

If you haven't already done so, making some kind of list or profile of the kind of person you think you'd like to date and get to know might be helpful. Your list could include four vertical columns. (This basic idea came from an article by Edra DeWitt "The Mr./Ms. Right Profile" in the magazine

Single Parent, December 1983.) The first column would be titled "Options to Consider." Included here might be traits you're looking for in relation to Activity, Appearance, Attraction, Communication Skills, Education, Status, Taste, Values, Religion, (and any others you can think of). The other three columns would be headed Like or Be, Not Like or Not Be, and Negotiable. Now take one of the broad terms and follow it horizontally across the other three columns. For example, take Activity. List in column two what kinds of activities you would hope this person would like or what characteristics the person should have (somewhat athletic, likes camping, symphony, or what?). List in column three the things you would not like (a traveler, a superjock, a homebody, or what?). Then in column four, list what might be negotiable. Do this with each of the broad terms and any others you can think of. This will at least help you zero in on some of the qualities important to you, and finding someone of like mind goes a long way in developing lasting relationships.

One caution: because you're looking for a particular person, don't let the process of looking rob you of being yourself. It's easy, I think, for some singles to get so wrapped up in looking that they forget to be themselves. Moving from a looking stance to a being stance is important because it allows you to cultivate your own interests and have a good time doing it. That affects your personality and that's what others see when they see you (more about this later).

The Meeting

A good profile, however, does not mean that this person will knock at your door one day and say, "Here, I am, I'm yours." One needs to know some strategies for meeting other people.

As I mentioned in another chapter, I remember an article sometime back that suggested that the first four minutes that strangers meet determines if they become acquaintances, friends, lifetime mates, or remain strangers. The contention was that four minutes was the amount of time strangers took to decide whether to part or to continue the encounter. To ensure some positive results, the article mentioned that if one displayed some confidence (born of a healthy self-esteem) and caring and a little consideration, one had a good chance of making the crucial four minutes work in one's favor.

This raises an important issue that we have to hurdle over if we're going to begin to learn how to meet other people successfully. It's so easy to lose out in those early moments of an encounter because we've made a judgment (usually based on appearance, as I said before) about the other person, even before he or she speaks. One of the first steps we need to take is to give other people a chance.

Another strategy that some singles have found helpful in bridging the stranger-friendship gap is to examine the desire to want to meet other people. Is it really there? Is it healthy? In other words, do you really want to meet new people for the pure fun and enjoyment of broadening your base of possible friends or do you just want to manipulate or use someone else for your gain or pleasure?

Exposure is another aspect of meeting new people. On a lonely evening we would like just to rub a genie lamp and have an instant friend appear and make the evening special. But it just doesn't happen that way. If I want to develop a special friendship, I have to get some exposure. I have to get out where people are. Some possibilities might be taking a class, joining a bowling league, working for a politician of your choice, attending single's seminars and workshops, getting involved in an exciting, growing church, or collecting for charity. These are only a few. Where will your interests take you?

Of course, just attending doesn't guarantee positive results. I have to display a friendly interest in other people and make some effort at conversation (a learned skill). If you're basically a shy person, you can work on that (see chapter 7 on friendship). You can usually start a conversation by simply introducing yourself and saying something about who you are, what you do for a living, or something about the activity. You can offer a sincere compliment, ask a question, or request some help or advice. The point is to make sure you start some kind of conversation. You don't want to stand around and wait for someone to talk to you. It's really not as hard as it would seem.

Here are some other ideas of activities and places to meet new people: go to museums, galleries, and malls; join a club (like a theater group or one related to your interests); participate in some sport or health facility; engage in some travel (there are now short-term cruises abbreviated to cut cost); design and submit a creative personal classified ad indicating the kind of person you'd like to meet (for help in creating the right one for you, check the personals in your local paper); accept those blind dates; check out "Dial-a-Date" (cost is one dollar a minute and can be seen advertized on TV as GABB or BLAB); check into Matchmakers (talk to someone who has called or used them); if you have a computer check out "Dial Your Match" from Computer Bulletin Board Systems; or you could also involve yourself in a Video Dating Service (the cost of $500 or $600 might be prohibitive for some and the risk of someone not wanting to meet you may also be a negative). This list is shared to acquaint you with what may be available to you in your area. It is not exhaustive nor is it recommended as the only way to go.

Places to Go and Things to Do

The following is only a partial list of possibilities to add to what has already been suggested or intimated. You and your date could

- Visit a zoo, shop at a mall, or browse in a bookstore.
- Go roller skating, horseback riding, canoeing, skiing, or biking.
- Organize a picnic (include friends or make it a special time for two).
- Volunteer together to help with a project (local or national).
- Wash and wax cars together.
- Read to each other.
- Plan an evening of games and popcorn with friends.
- Prepare a big pot of soup together and invite some friends to enjoy it with you.
- Play a mutual sport together followed with a meal.
- Paint a picture or write a story together.
- Put a jigsaw puzzle together (a big one).
- Earn some money together (refinish furniture, weave a rug, can and sell some fruit or vegetables).
- Have a progressive dinner (together plan and visit different restaurants, one for salad, one for soup, one for the main course, and still another for dessert).
- Visit a shut-in (see your pastor if you need help).
- Go to an auction or a yard or garage sale or flee market.

- Attend a musical event.
- Take your cameras and create a photo essay (public library can provide help).
- Spend an evening at the library and conclude with a special dessert.
- Take a walk in the rain.
- Attend a lecture or take a course together.

As suggested earlier, this is only a partial list but it may have stimulated some other ideas you thought about as you read through it.

How Do You Know It's Love

Let's assume that you have been dating for a while. You're getting to know the other person fairly well. You feel you have moved from being acquaintances to real friends. You're beginning to wonder whether this is love, infatuation, or what. One process that could help you determine the difference is to work through the following list known as "The Big Ten" suggested by Sol Gordon in his book *The Teenage Survival Book* in a chapter titled "Toward a Successful Marriage." Even though the book was written for teen-agers, this list has some significant thoughts for all ages. The list is complied in order of importance.

Some indicators of mature love:
1. Caring, intimacy, loyalty, and trust are present (honest caring for the other person).
2. Learning how and when to laugh (sense of humor in the relationship).

3. Making interesting conversation (open communication).
4. Togetherness, a passionate sense of mission about something (a concerted effort to do meaningful activities together).
5. Maintaining friendships both together and separately (freedom to maintain important relationships with other people).
6. Promising not to compromise the person you want to be (an understanding of the other's point of view without having to agree).
7. Tolerating irritability, tiredness, clumsiness, and memory lapse (mood swings are acknowledged as part of life).
8. Willingness to accept each other's style (a feeling that both are accepted for who they are, active or passive, extrovert or introvert, or whatever).
9. Sexual fulfillment (intimacy needs of all kinds being met, not necessarily sexual intercourse).
10. Sharing household tasks (a desire to do whatever tasks may need to be done, regardless of what male and female roles have suggested as "normal" in the past).

As you can see, these are ingredients for a happy and successful marriage. One significant observation Dr. Gordon makes is that sexual fulfillment, **without the first eight ingredients**, is nothing more than mechanics and has very little meaning. It just becomes something you do. In other words, if there is no indication of a commitment to this kind of love, then this lack becomes an important reason for leaving sexual activity out.

Coping When Not Dating

We can live our lives using a number of approaches. Let's look at two as we consider times when we're not dating. One approach says in effect, I have to act, prove, and do the best I can. The feeling is that I have to use a system to manipulate or control. I always have to be strong and gain my strength from doing, always impressing others. I have to show the appearance of perfection. I do this by doing what is expected. I try hard to avoid any consequences of being myself; because of that I find myself defending or regretting the past and fearing the future.

Another approach says in effect: I have to **be** as genuine as I can be. I can express who I am, accepting my strengths and weaknesses, my joys and sorrows. I can, as I open myself for self-evaluation, build a respect for who I am with the gifts and talents I have. I can be aware of, and express in nonjudgemental ways, my feelings. In other words, it's okay to be me. Criticism is welcome and leads to growth. I can learn to trust and be myself as fully as possible, **now**.

The point here is that I can move from doing to being. If I'm not dating and I feel I want to be or should be, I can work hard at being the best me possible. I can move from a doing, acting, proving stance to a being stance. I can take who I truly believe myself to be into future relationships and let the chips fall where they may. Whether I'm dating or not, the one sure thing I can concentrate on is being me. Being who you are **first** and letting what you do be governed by that being will take you into areas of interest and self-improvement, places you want to serve, sights you want to see. When you meet someone of the opposite sex wherever your being takes you, you can assume that they, too, are interested in the same kind of experiences you are—a terrific base from which to start a relationship. And if one doesn't happen, at least you're doing what you want to do.

Saying No

This occurs at different times. We'll examine at least two: when you don't want to go out with a person asking for a date and when sex becomes an issue.

Saying no to a date should be based on some obvious differences. You know, for example, your moral stance, your interest in places to go, and activities you like to do. You may not be aware of where this other person stands. You may want to accept or suggest meeting him or her at a restaurant for coffee so you can get some more information. If the realization becomes obvious to you that the person asking you out is at the opposite end of where you're coming from, then it also should be obvious that an evening with that person would be a disaster. Saying no should be as easy as "I'm sorry, but I have other plans." Other plans could always include cleaning the house or apartment (which wouldn't be a lie).

Saying no to sex should be based on well-thought-out reasons that you've come to in your attempt to be the kind of moral person you want to be. Jim Smoke tells the story of a girl he was counseling who told him of a date she had the previous night. She said they had gone to dinner and a movie. On the way home he said to her, "Well, should we spend the night at my place or yours?" Her response was one of total indignation and she felt compelled to tell him in no uncertain terms that she wasn't that kind of a woman. At the next traffic light she got out of the car and slammed the door and walked home. After hearing the story, Jim's comment to her indicated there might have been a better response. Taken back, she asked him what he meant. He told her she could have used the opportunity to explain why she felt as she did and maybe give the other person something to think about.

Have you thought out your reasons? The next chapter might be of help if you haven't.

Being single does not mean you failed at intimacy, just as being married does not mean you succeeded.

The Reality of Intimacy

Let me open this chapter by saying I am not going to propose an easy solution for you. I am not going to advocate the position that because you are a worthy follower of Jesus Christ your sexuality is always neatly in place without any problems. I am not going to suggest that relating to your sexuality and its expression is no big deal and can be easily summed up with either "you do or you don't." I am not going to give anyone permission to do whatever with whoever whenever. I don't have that right or power. I am not going to say that the Bible is full of concrete examples of how single adults should express their sexuality. (In fact, if you were to become a biblical scholar in the truest sense of that profession you would find that the Bible shows a limited interest in our sexual agendas. Its overall main concern is the conversion and commitment of individuals to Jesus Christ, which produces salvation. Salvation makes a difference in the way we respond to our own lives and the lives of others, and one of the major differences is our responsibility to share that salvation with others.) I am not going to say that if you have problems and concerns with intimacy needs it's because you haven't prayed hard enough about it. (Nothing wrong with prayer, but it can become a glib way of suggesting that there's nothing to this, and all you have to do is get a hold of God and all will be well.) I am not going to assume that everyone is going to agree with everything in this chapter. I simply trust the process and your intellect to take what's for you and let it instruct you in your pilgrimage and leave the rest for someone else.

What we're discussing in this chapter is a serious, sensitive, and I believe, misunderstood **gift** we've all been given to enjoy. I am not going to minimize the struggle, but I am going to strongly advocate our coming to believe we're not in the struggle alone.

What I am going to explore in this chapter is (1) a workable definition of intimacy and its relation to our sexuality, celibacy, and friendships; (2) some choices we have to express our sexual desires; (3) some **must** reading on this subject (books and ideas that have challenged and influenced my thoughts and directions on this subject); and (4) a working definition of the kind of intimacy we need.

I trust that what follows will suggest to you that I'm keenly aware of the struggle (having been single now for some fifteen years after seventeen years of marriage) and have attempted to review the alternatives honestly and answer some of the questions as appropriately as I can.

Intimacy Defined

The reality of intimacy is that we all need and want it. Life relating to life in intimate ways helps us understand how better to live the gift of life we've been given. We learn from one another as we interrelate with one another.

The concern, however, seems to be that many single adults have bought into what our culture has promoted as the normal ingredients for true intimacy to happen.

Webster defines intimacy as "a state of being in a close, friendly association or personal relationship with someone, marked by love or affection and a depth of knowledge and information about this person." In the process of relating an interweaving of personalities occurs. Webster also suggests that the word implies "a sexual liberty taken." In my dictionary there's no further explanation of what that means, so my interpretation is that intimacy insinuates that a physical contact can be part of intimacy which may or may not be sexual intercourse.

Edward E. Thornton says in an article titled "Intimacy in the Christian Life" (*Review and Expositor*, March, 1982) that intimacy is "a quality of openness in relation to one's self and others that leads to a state of being respectful of and committed to sharing in common with oneself and others."

What is intimacy? True, it has sexual connotations but it is much more that that. It's an openness to life that helps us understand what relating to ourselves and to others means. I believe it is also an openness that helps us understand and relate to God as well. God has to be involved in our definition because God desires to be in relation to us, so that we enjoy God's presense, wisdom, strength, and mercy. As we open ourselves to God in honest and truthful ways, we find honesty and truthfulness becoming part of our response to ourselves and others, and honesty and truthfulness bring intimacy into our lives. Hence, intimacy is a quality that is developed and never completely or fully grasped. It involves us sexually because we are sexual, but it is much more than physical. When intimacy is part of our lives, part of our friendships, we begin to understand and appreciate more and more the beauty and importance of our own lives and life in general. We begin to understand and appreciate more and more the lives we "touch" physically, intellectually, and emotionally. We begin to understand and appreciate more and more our personal relationship with God and God's plan for our lives.

Intimacy is not something we possess overnight or something "out there" to be picked off the shelf of life's options at random. **It cannot be part of casual relationships**. It cannot evolve where there is a closed self-centered, self-reliant, self-depreciating spirit. In other words, intimacy cannot happen to a person who by intent or otherwise says to others "I don't need anybody" or "I'll do it myself" or "I'll do it my way." It cannot happen to a person who is constantly putting himself or herself down. It cannot happen to a person who lives a selfish, egotistical, narcissistic life that constantly asks "What's in it for **me**?" And, of course, it cannot happen to one who defines intimacy narrowly as exclusively a sexual encounter.

To be sure it's far easier to define than achieve, but intimacy, the kind we need, is possible (with or without intercourse).

Intimacy and Sexuality

The information we get from television, the best sellers on the New York Times list, the movies, and modern music is that these two words are synonymous. The suggestion is that the kind of intimacy we need is reached through an expression and satisfaction of our sexual desires. Whether we're married or not is irrelevant. Our culture's point of view has led us to believe that sexuality is what we do rather than what we are.

Although they are related, they are not synonymous, however. Since we've defined intimacy earlier in the chapter, how then should we define this everpresent power and desire that's part of being a physical human being, called sexuality?

1. Let's first establish that our sexuality is God's idea.

As such, it cannot be considered inherently evil. It's God's gift and God has great purpose and interest in this dimension of our humanity. God created us in the image that was God's own, "In the image of God he created . . . ; male and female he created them . . . [and a few verses later] God saw all that he had made, and it was very good" (Genesis 1:27, 31).

2. Our sexuality has to do with being, knowing, and enjoying who we are as female and male.

After being born male or female, we take on our roles as male or female from models we had growing up (parents, guardians, peers, heroes, and heroines). So, we come to decide that it's either okay or not okay to be male or female. There's no way that I can be more masculine than I am at this moment. I was born male. It's not what I do. It's what I am. So our sexuality has to do with our roles as male and female. At the present time these roles have been changing, for better or worse. The meaning is not as clear as it once was concerning what being male and female means. In the movies John Wayne has been replaced by a Dustin Hoffman, who shows us a different kind of hero. The homemaker role has been replaced with women climbing the corporate ladder and becoming more sexually aggressive. This leaves some confusion in its wake. But as we define or redefine our roles we are dealing with our sexuality.

3. Our sexuality is involved in all of our personality. Some would say that at least four dimensions characterize our personality:

a. Biological (meaning physical, having muscles, veins and arteries, senses, size, and the like).

b. Emotional (capable of feeling love and hate, sexual desire, joy and sorrow, and so forth).

c. Intellectual (capable of thinking, making decisions and choices).

d. Spiritual (being born in the image of God we are privileged to be in partnership with God).

Because we are all of this and more (we could add social and relational), we can't isolate these from one another. They are all part of the whole. What we do with our physical dimension affects the other dimensions. Hence, our sexuality is more than physical.

4. Our sexuality leads us into relationships.

Through attraction and stimulation our sexuality draws us into relationships. For some their sexuality leads them into relationships in which talking, listening, and being heard are essential. Because of who they are, where they may be in their personal pilgrimage, and their devotion to their value system, talking, listening, and being heard can satisfy some intimacy needs. For these people sexual contact beyond this is not the way their sexuality needs to be expressed. For others, "touch" might be added. The kind of touch would involve a genuine warm hug that suggests caring and support. We do this well at funerals but not so well elsewhere. Just to be held in someone's tender caring arms can go a long way toward supplying some of our intimacy needs. Now, I'm not suggesting that we be naive enough to assume that this could not lead to something more stimulating, but it doesn't have to.

What we're talking about here is platonic friendships. Two people of the opposite sex can enjoy each other's friendship without having sexual intercourse. I guess in one sense they are like a brother-sister relationship—not unlike what was meant by the church when we called each other brother and sister. Maybe the church needs to resurrect the deeper meanings of these words to help us better define our sexuality, whether we're married or single. These kinds of friendships do not satisfy the desire for sexual intercourse but they can meet some of our intimacy needs.

For others, who see their intimacy needs solely connected to their physical sexuality, the touching leads to a network of decisions and arousal that, if continued, builds toward and culminates in sexual intercourse. This could lead one to an attitude that says sex is okay anytime, anyplace, with anybody. The physical aspect of sexuality is satisfied, but, again, there are no guarantees that other aspects of our intimacy needs will also be met. In fact, some may even be circumvented.

So, intimacy and sexuality are related but not synonymous. When our sexuality is seen as purely physical, one aspect of intimacy may be satisfied, but we still may not feel the deeper meanings of its broader definition.

Intimacy and Celibacy

As the word *celibacy* is mentioned, certain questions immediately surface: Can anyone live a celibate life in today's world? Do I want to live a celibate life? Can single adults be celibate and still find intimacy? How can single adults today develop affectionate but nonsexual friendships with the opposite sex?

If we accept the earlier definition of intimacy as valid, then we can conclude that yes, we can. Naturally, the intimacy is qualified because the physical aspect of our sexuality is not expressed in sexual intercourse. However, if in our relationships with others (of both sexes) we can develop an openness that's based on honesty and truthfulness, we can experience intimacy that can meet some of our needs. Of course this assumes that both the people involved accept the definition and abide by it.

If we can be open to God and God's plan for our lives and enjoy God's presence and strength, then we can experience an intimacy and friendship with God. As that relationship develops, our lives are enriched with faith, hope, and love. We then carry these attributes into our relationships with others. Learning to love God with all our heart, mind, soul, and strength better equips us to love others in ways that embrace life.

Obviously the New Testament clearly recognizes both marriage and a celibate lifestyle as acceptable for believers in Christ.

Jesus lifted marriage to a high plane saying, "What God has joined together, let man not separate" (Matthew 19:6). He spoke against easy divorce and having as many sexual partners as you want, and, yet at the same time, Jesus lived a celibate life without asceticism. He freely involved himself with the world of women and men. He didn't crawl into a cave or live in a monastery. In the same chapter in which he elevated marriage (Matthew 19) he also said that not everyone was meant for marriage. Some will be eunuchs he said. He didn't explain his celibacy, he just lived it. He didn't comment on Genesis 2:18 ("It is not good for the man to be alone"), a text that suggests that one should seek to be married. Why, we don't know. What he did do was to be totally caught up in his call to the ministry of salvation. This freed him of the responsibility of a family, a house, or a secure job and enabled him to teach, heal, travel, and reach as many people as he could.

His remarks about lusting are clear. He suggested it produced bad sex. "I tell you that anyone who looks at a woman lustfully [the Greek here suggests with strong desire, the kind that produces action] has already committed adultery with her in his heart" (Matthew 5:28). We know what he thought about adultery.

"Lust produces bad sex, because it denies relationship. Lust turns the other person into an object, a thing, a nonperson. Jesus condemned lust because it cheapened sex, it makes sex less than it was created to be."[1] The kind of lust that makes people objects to be used is in direct opposition to the kind of love and respect Jesus intended his followers to have for one another. People were always more important than things to Jesus. The kind of lust I believe Jesus was talking about has to do with an uncontrolled sexual passion that leads one to be a taker, not a giver.

Paul too, speaks highly of both marriage and celibacy. In 1 Corinthians 7, both are mentioned as valid life-styles. It's obvious however, that he leans toward celibacy, and there are some possible reasons for this. The passage suggests that at the time of this writing he, too, was celibate, and so he was speaking out of his own experience. But there is also the feeling of urgency in the letter. He felt that the end was coming soon and one could serve God better as a single (one wouldn't have all the responsibilities marriage creates).

For Paul, celibacy was a worthy life-style for any Christian who believed he or she had the gift for its demands (1 Corinthians 7:7, 17-24). Clearly not everyone has the gift. One who despises his or her singleness and feels overwhelmingly that he or she must be married obviously would not be so gifted. Conversely, any Christian single adult who feels no constraint to marry, exercises self-control, and is anxious about the affairs of the Lord and how to please him in body and spirit could assume he or she is so gifted for the moment. For the moment, because gifts can change just as people can. I don't believe God locks anyone into a certain life-style for life.

For Paul, the concern was with freedom—freedom that is possible for anyone living in "undivided devotion to God." This was his goal—to give himself so totally to God through Jesus Christ that his life-style was a "praise to God." He wrote his letter to the Corinthians hoping to instill this kind of devotion. I don't believe he believed a married person couldn't live this way, but he did believe it would be easier for a single person.

So, what have we said so far? God created the world and everything in it, including our sexuality, and what God has created is good. We have been created to enjoy God and the way God has made us male and female. Our sexuality is part of who we are, and it is a gift from God. The misuse of the gift is prevalent. Sexual immorality as well as "idolatry and witchcraft, hatred, discord, jealousy, fits of rage, selfish ambition"and more (Galatians 5:20), all get in the way of our enjoying

God and Jesus Christ. On the other hand, Jesus Christ and our devotion to him and his way of life, can free us from the obstacles.

So, the issue is not so much how far I can go or how long I remain celibate. For Paul, the issue was devotion to Christ. If that is central, then our sexual behavior is not centered on rules but on devotion to Christ and his cause. The question becomes, Can I move to a devotion to Jesus Christ that is so intense and close and intimate that regardless of the situation I will do the loving thing—the one that will enhance my devotion and I hope enhance others in their devotion as well.

Granted, it's not easy, but I believe we can conclude that with God's help it is possible.

The Kind of Intimacy We Need

Society has equated, whether rightly or wrongly, intimacy with sexual intercourse. Even though Webster suggests it to be part of the definition, many have assumed it to be the only definition. Terry Hershey's book *Beginning Again* says it well: "As long as we assume that the issue of intimacy is resolved with sensual touch, then we avoid the real work of honesty, communication, conflict resolution, and commitment. Neither a sexual encounter nor marriage guarantees intimacy."[2] Just because one has a sexual encounter doesn't mean one has had an intimate relationship. Just because one is married doesn't mean one has had an intimate relationship, either.

So, what kind of intimacy do we need? The kind of intimacy we need is the kind that

• Helps us honestly be open to a healthy relationship with ourselves. This kind motivates us to be present to ourselves in an appreciative way that is thankful for the gift of life, which includes our sexuality.

• Helps us realize that loneliness is often the culprit that drives us into sexual encounters. The kind of intimacy that vigorously attempts to find and appropriate positive, workable, healthy ways to deal with loneliness.

• Gently moves us into the presence of others with a sense of security that expresses itself in an open posture and countenance that says, "It's okay to be me."

• Works hard at changing the sexual aspect of it from a need to a want. I need food, water, air to live. They are not something I want, they are necessities. On the other hand I don't need sexual intercourse to stay alive. I may want it, but I do not need it.

• Cultivates making effective communication a primary goal. Effective communication involves skills in listening and sharing with others in nonjudgemental ways our feelings, ideas, dreams, and goals, all of which produce intimacy. Skills can be learned. If whatever communication skills I now have and use are not working, I can unlearn inadequate ones and relearn ones that will serve future relationships effectively.

• Most important, this kind of intimacy motivates us to enjoy God freely, urges us to love God wholeheartedly, and commits us to grow in God's presence daily.

Concluding Remarks

When all is said and done, some tough choices have to be made regarding our sexual expression. How you decide and what you decide has to be your personal choice and decision. I trust that whatever your personal choice is, it will be influenced by an accurate definition of intimacy and a workable understanding of biblical principle.

Christian single adults can make a tremendous contribution here. The more we're able to concentrate on making a significant contribution with our lives, making a difference because we're motivated by a relentless drive to serve God, the more we can feel good about who we are and where we are. The more we are able to live lives that enjoy God's presence and power, the less we may be overwhelmed by low self-esteem, loneliness, and that everpresent powerful gift called sexuality.

---

[1]Richard Foster, *Money, Sex, and Power* (San Francisco, CA: Harper & Row, 1985), 99.

[2]Terry Hershey, *Beginning Again*, (Nashville, TN: Thomas Nelson, 1986), 95.

Dear John,
I look forward to our wedding, I do.
It may take longer than we had
first calculated, though, since I now
think it would be best to wait until
you are the last man on earth.

Sincerely,
Janice

The Reality of Breaking Up

In some relationships the fact becomes obvious that no matter how sincere the effort to patch it up and continue as usual, is present, the intensity of the struggle to continue is so painful that the only recourse is to break off the relationship.

In this chapter we will take a serious look at when and how that is done and what might be some of the ramifications. We will be exploring loss in general and how to deal with it long term.

George had been seeing Helen now for some time. They have gotten fairly well acquainted, knowing each other's likes and dislikes, and so on. But George was beginning to notice some feelings that he was experiencing. He couldn't put his finger on exactly what the problem was, but he just knew the relationship wasn't going anywhere, and he felt he had to do something. What to do, however, was a big problem.

Ever feel like that? Maybe you find yourself in that situation as you read this. What do you do when you find you are no longer interested in continuing the relationship? How do you "get off the bus, Gus" or "get out the back, Jack?"

Probably one of the first considerations is to look at some indicators that help us determine whether or not a relationship is going sour. In addition to our own feelings we could add

1. Loss of interest causing lack of meaningful communication.

2. Lack of responsibility and respect.

3. The desire to change the other person.

4. Breaking up and making up, over and over, again and again.

5. The feeling that the situation will be different when we're married.

6. Lack of basic agreement on basic issues (money, children, church, and so forth).

7. Those close to you are suggesting you need to ask yourself whether you really want to spend the rest of your life with this person.

8. The feeling that you're not growing, that you are even being prevented from growing.

9. Of course, even the slightest provocation of physical or other abuse (you don't need anybody who can't control his or her temper enough to keep his/her hands off you).

When any of these enter a relationship, it's a good sign that your must discuss them. Priority time and effort ought to be given to see if any resolution can be found. But if a satisfactory solution isn't possible, then plans should be made to break off the relationship.

How, then, does one leave a relationship with dignity, trusting that both parties involved retain their self-worth and can move on with some sense of courage into future relationships, using what was learned from previous ones to their advantage?

Naturally, a lot depends on the two people involved.

You could do what one woman did. She knew that the relationship wasn't going anywhere for her, so she sent her boyfriend a cactus plant. When he received it he was with some friends. He told them that they had had an argument the night before and that she was probably sending him an apology. When he opened the envelope with the card in it, he found the message in big red letters, "Sit on it."

Some up-front guidelines for a different approach might include these: communicate one on one, face to face (not over the phone or by letter); avoid put-downs and manipulation; stick to your reasons and feelings; and do your best to remember that you are not evil, inadequate, or incompetent because a relationship has failed.

In some instances, no matter what positive attempts are made at easing out of a relationship, the party who wants the relationship to continue will experience some form of rejection and the pain that follows (low self-esteem because he or she may feel something must be wrong with them). Their reaction to it all can leave them devastated. No one likes rejection, but you have no control over the way another responds to it. You would hope that the person will accept your reasoning and be able as soon as is feasible for them to get on with building future relationships. What you can do is to make sure the other party hears and understands your reasons for wanting out. To the best of your ability that person needs to hear (whether he or she accepts it or not) that it's the relationship you're rejecting, not the person. This, of course, is not easily distinguishable to the party wanting to continue. Again, you cannot do much other than express your reasons.

Some thoughts to keep in mind: Do I need to develop some skills to express my feelings in nonjudgemental terms? If so, these skills can be learned. It is my life, my future. What I do with the present does affect that future. If a relationship isn't working today and nothing has been resolved, it probably won't be working later. What we do with our lives is important. We are not for everyone and everyone is not for us.

What if you're the one who wants the relationship to continue? If you've been as sincere as you know how to reconcile the differences and have tried to recreate part of the delightful times once shared, and the struggle brings nothing but pain, it's probably best to move as quickly as possible to accepting reality. If you feel rejection, you'll need to work extra hard at building your self-esteem (see chapters four and five). Remembering past rejections might be helpful. You've felt the pain of rejection at an earlier time in your life. All of us have. Can you remember how you handled it then? What did you do that was helpful? Can you stay away from reactions that were harmful? You've also experienced loss before. How did you survive then? How did you let healing take place? How were you able to put the past in the past? How did you "let go"? Who helped you "let go"?

Some other steps you might take to help ease the transition: permit yourself to grieve (after all there has been the loss of a relationship); avoid activities that remind you of former experiences with that person; plan for concrete and creative ways to meet new people; start or continue worthwhile projects (exercise, hobby, taking a class); and, though it may be painful at first, do your best to cut off contact.

In other words, put the past in proper perspective. As quickly as possible leave what's over without denying its importance. If it has been a long relationship, some significant experiences have happened. In the sharing of your time, dreams, and energy, you gave something of yourself to another. In the give and take you learned something about yourself. Relationships work that way. What has been learned will be a benefit in future relationships.

In fact, if you can move toward seeing the relationship as a forerunner to future relationships, you have come a long way in putting it in proper perspective. For example, we know that for various reasons, we outgrow relationships. There's nothing wrong with that nor do we intend to put down anyone else with some smug arrogance. It happens. When it does we need to keep it in perspective. We owe something to our past relationships. They brought us to where we are. They are forerunners and we need to accept them with sufficient humility.

It's like what happened to the relationship between John the Baptist and Jesus. John was the forerunner. He came before Jesus to help pave the way for his coming. He wasn't the long-awaited Messiah. Many of our relationships are like that: forerunners for future relationships.

Just a few closing remarks about loss in general: Throughout our lives we will continue to experience loss. We gain some friends and lose them. We have children and soon they're on their own. We gain some strength and lose it. We get use to a house and a neighborhood and then move. We work hard for our money then lose our purse or wallet. We give our best to a job and then are told we're not needed anymore. Our usual response to all this loss is "If only I would have . . ." or "What if. . . ." Instead, we need to build the fact of loss into our thinking and consider some ways to deal with it.

After any loss we have to reevaluate and buy into a new future. That begs the question, Can I? Part of the answer to that lies in our understanding of the grief process and some fundamental ways we deal with the stress it causes. Now for the one who has initiated the breakup, little or no grief therapy may be needed. Dealing with some guilt and stress, however, will be present. Loss shatters whatever security we've built up in the relationship. It threatens balance that we've gotten use to, and it can cause a sense of confusion. Because of all this, we react. Normal reactions to loss include shock, maybe some physical symptoms (tightness in the throat, empty feeling in the stomach, weakness, and the like), sense of isolation, panic, and hostility. One may have difficulty returning to normal affairs of life. But hope returns gradually and then readjustment to the new. Here are some steps to take:

1. Remember that it is important to cry freely as you feel the need.

2. Be patient with yourself.

3. Realize that socialization may be difficult for a while.

4. Remember to care for your body by giving it nourishing food, rest, exercise, and sunshine.

5. As much as is possible, talk with people when you need to do so.

6. Acknowledge the normal reaction to loss.

Loss causes stress and stress makes us feel uneasy. It can, in time, cause high blood pressure, ulcers, and even premature death. If you know that stress is causing a negative reaction in your life because of your loss, seeking the advice of your doctor or psychiatrist may be important. Some ways to cope with stress include the following:

I. Learn to accept what you cannot change.

2. Learn the art of meditation and relaxation.

3. Avoid self-medication (drugs of any kind don't teach you how to cope with stress).

4. Set small, reachable goals for yourself (reaching them will bring a sense of control)

5. As much as is possible, share your concerns with someone you love, trust, or respect.

The loss of a relationship can take its toll on our system both physically and emotionally. You can, however, come through the experience a better person. Painful as it may be, it can be a positive force that actually can be, as one looks back on it from a distant perspective, the motivation one needed to accept an exciting new future.

Would you be better married or single? On what are you basing your answer?

The Reality of a Future Marriage

How real is it? I once overheard this statement at a Creative Single's Workshop: "Anyone can get married if he or she wants to be married badly enough." Maybe so. The statement implies, I assume, that if you were asked by (or if you asked) enough people to marry you, someone would eventually consent. But that fosters a follow-up question: Would that someone be the right one for you? Maybe and maybe not.

Some other questions, if answered honestly, can help us determine whether marriage or a single life-style may be in our future (for the moment at least). The answers to them will make up the content of this chapter. They are, Are you marriageable material? Would you be better off single (for now)? What is an effective marriage, and can one be a reality for you? What about remarriage? Suppose you don't marry?

Are You Marriageable Material?

Some assumptions will be made before we attempt an answer: (1) You believe you have the necessary communication skills needed to develop an effective relationship, and (2) you are willing to date.

Single adults have a good chance of being ready for a marital relationship if they, as Christians, feel and believe that God would be pleased with them if they were married.

We know that the Bible suggests both the married life and the single life as viable options for human beings. How do you know God's option for you? I believe prayer plays an important part here, honestly laying out before God, your sincere desire to know God's will. We have assurances that that kind of prayer will be answered. God promises it. As this desire takes hold, I believe it will become obvious to us what God wants for us. If a certain person comes into our lives, the attraction is there, and events seem to be leading toward commitment, marriage could be the obvious choice. I believe God's wisdom and strength will be available to make our lives fulfilling and happy. If that certain someone doesn't appear, I believe, God's wisdom and strength is also available to help us live a happy, satisfying single life. Either way, I can be fulfilled. With God, I can live a rewarding, challenging life, whether I'm single or married.

Single adults have a good chance of being ready for a marital relationship if they are learning to adjust to change.

You've heard it said by one person of a

married couple: "He [she] is not the man [woman] I married." Naturally we hope, whether we're married or single, we're not the same person we were a year ago or five years ago. We hope, we've grown in positive ways. Regardless, life and God (if we've submitted ourselves to God) don't leave us the same. We all change, and we need to build that into our future thinking. This is one of the areas about marriage that makes it scary. We have no guarantee that the person we intend to marry will change for the better or worse. We can assume they will change. One way we might help ourselves, however, is to make sure that whatever courtship we have is long enough to determine whether or not this person has the desire to grow in positive ways. Some indicators of that might include a love for reading, an inquisitive mind, one who appreciates seminars, workshops, and similar growth-producing activities.

Single adults enhance their chances of being ready for a marital relationship if they are whole persons.

Being whole has to do with learning to enjoy your own company. Enjoying our own company helps us realize we can be whole in who we are as single adults. I'm not suggesting a narcissistic, self-centered lifestyle. What I think is important is a healthy regard for one's strengths and weaknesses, one's uniqueness, one's talents and interests. Single adults are whole when they come to realize that it's okay to be married and it's okay to be single. They are not, however, assuming that marriage will make them whole. They believe they can live happily as a married person or happily as a single person. They are also aware that because they can live happily with themselves, their likelihood of living happily with someone else is much better.

Single adult enhance their likelihood of being ready for a marital relationship if they are learning how to adjust to another person's life-style and personality.

They realize the beauty of diversity, knowing that no two people are exactly alike. They can accept others for who they are without having to change them. They can live and let live. This doesn't mean, however, that they agree with wrong behavior. Instead, they have come to some understanding about their own personality and what provided the experiences that influenced it, and they realize that others have their own histories that made them who they are.

If you're really getting serious about someone and feel you need some help in understanding his or her personality, many couples have taken and found the Taylor-Johnson Temperament Analysis or the Myers-Briggs Type Indicator to be extremely helpful. These inventories help focus on personality traits and their relationship to one another. These are available at most colleges and universities for a nominal fee.

Single adults enhance their likelihood of being ready for a marital relationship if they know and believe that they just can't live alone.

They have lived alone long enough to know that their personality would be happier shared with someone else. I believe, however, "lived alone long enough" means a minimum of two years for those who have been suddenly made single by death or divorce. Naturally, in the early stages of transition, a formerly married person will experience the loneliness more acutely and could interpret that as justifying their urgent feelings of wanting to find someone to spend the rest of their lives with in an intimate relationship. But as one adjusts to the new life-style, some positives will begin to emerge, after which one can make a better assessment of one's feelings. Besides, after a tragedy like death or divorce, you need time to sort out your options, to answer that all-important question: Who am I, now that I'm no longer in a marriage? If you've never married, then you're familiar with the positives and negatives of the life-style. It then becomes a matter of accepting the reality of a single life and living it to the full. However, when the pain of the negatives in the single life-style becomes greater than the fear of the future and a risk is taken to change the situation, it might be an indicator that you just can't live alone anymore.

Would You Be Better Off Single (for now)?

One way to look at this would be to list

some of the wrong reasons for wanting to get married. If your reasons for marriage falls into any of the following, you might be wise to reevaluate your decision. You would indeed be better off single, because to start a partnership based on these reasons could be disastrous. They cannot contribute to building an effective, productive, healthy marriage (which will be discussed in the next section).

You want to marry

1. Because you need to fill a void (sexual or otherwise) in your life;

2. Because you want to get even with your former spouse;

3. Because you want to be healed emotionally;

4. Because you want to become a whole person;

5. Because this person is just like your former spouse or girlfriend or boyfriend;

6. Because you believe that being unhappily married is better then not being married at all;

7. Because you hate being single.

What Is an Effective Marriage and Can One Be a Reality for You?

Sometime back I remember reading an article in *Savvy* magazine that listed some of the basic ingredients that went into developing and maintaining a successful business partnership. A number of successful partners were interviewed and from the interviews came this partial list: open communication, respect (able to tolerate each other's mistakes), dedication to goals both have agreed are beneficial. There were others but I think these give you a flavor of their conclusions. The chemistry of a business partnership seems to require a delicate mixture of individual skills, cooperative efforts, and mutual respect. These seem to me to be some of the effective ingredients that go into a happy, healthy marriage. In fact, looking at marriage as a partnership seems to me to be a very realistic approach.

In that light, questions come to mine: Do I really want to be in a partnership with somebody else? In any partnership, two ingredients for success surface as important: cooperation and compromise. Do I understand these terms and if I do, am I willing to let them be an active part of the relationship (accepting the responsibility for making the partnership the way I want it)? Am I willing to discuss differing points of view? Is "negotiation" a part of my relational style? (If not, *Getting to Yes: Negotiating Agreement Without Giving In* by Roger Fisher and William Ury could be of tremendous help). Since we are moving toward more equality in marriages with the changing of roles, can I live with a situation with no one person "in charge" and no one winning or losing? This implies some hard work in communication. Am I willing and ready to make marriage a priority (meaning lifetime commitment)? Do I have or am I willing to learn effective communication skills (which imply self-discipline, time, and effort)?

Some further factors that constitute an effective marriage partnership would include a faith in God and Jesus Christ and in your partner's good intentions (this is at the heart of true trust); a full acceptance and appreciation of one's own worth as a person (which allows you to be your own genuine self) and the worth of your partner; a wholesome attitude about sexuality and its expression; a commitment to promote the positive growth of each partner (physically, intellectually, emotionally, socially, spiritually); and a marriageable mind-set.

A marriageable mind-set recognizes that our freedom to be ourselves is important. For some that freedom may have been discouraged. As we grew up we may have heard from our parents or peers that it wasn't okay to be ourselves. We may have heard and believed that we shouldn't feel, think for ourselves, be ourselves, trust anyone, grow up (leave mommy and daddy), accept our sexuality, and on and on. A marriageable mind-set gives one permission to exchange or replace these with positive statements which, of course, are the reverse. "I can be who I am, I can think and solve problems, I can be close with someone of the opposite sex, I can trust other people." If you have lived your life as a codependent (always letting others tell you who you are and where to go and what to do), it will interfere with your ability to become an effective marriage partner. If this is your concern you will find Melody Beattie's book *Beyond Codependency and Getting Better All the Time* most helpful.

What about Remarriage?

Does the reality of a future marriage exist for those who were once married but are now single again? If your spouse died, the question can be answered biblically by Paul's words to the Corinthians. They suggest freedom to remarry to anyone whose spouse had died (1 Corinthians 7:39-40). Paul's directive, however, was that those who found themselves suddenly made single by death would remarry someone who belonged "to the Lord." He did, however, conclude that a widow (widower) would be happier if she (he) stayed single. His explanation of why is because of the present crisis (v. 26), time is short (v. 29), this world in its present form is passing away, and Paul would like people to be free from the concerns and responsibilities of marriage (vv. 31-32), so that you can live in undivided devotion to the Lord (v. 35).

If, on the other hand, you are divorced the answer is not as clear. Biblically, we know God hates divorce (Malachi 2:16). He hates it because of what it does to people. He hates it because of what it does to families and children. He hates it because it disrupts the ideal of marriage, promoted in God's Word. The New Testament ideal for marriage is one man, one wife, for life. But, as we are painfully aware, the ideal isn't always reality. People are human and make human responses that interfere with ideals.

Biblical scholars of all stripes have differing opinions about what the Bible says about divorce and remarriage. There are those at one end of the continuum who espouse no divorce, anytime, for anybody, anywhere, under any circumstances (which excludes any reason for remarriage). At the other end would be those who would say "Yes, there is divorce, and yes, there is remarriage anytime, anyplace, for anybody." In between are other positions: Yes, there is divorce, but not remarriage for any reason; yes, there is divorce and remarriage, but not for anybody or at any time. It's okay for the "innocent" party to remarry (innocent may be hard to determine) or it's only okay to remarry if you hold out until your former spouse remarries because then there is no chance of reconciliation. The scholars who support these opinions can back up their reasoning with biblical insight.

Where does that leave us? **To do some searching ourselves**. The major passages that must be considered for formulating a position are:

Genesis 2:4-25

Deuteronomy 24:1-4
Matthew 5:31-32; 19:1-12
Mark 10:1-12
Luke 16:18
1 Corinthians 7:1-16

For your study I would recommend some good commentaries, a Bible dictionary, and a concordance. I would also recommend the following books: *Divorce and Remarriage in the Bible* by Kenneth Jones; *Remarriage: A Healing Gift from God* by Larry Richards; *Marriage, Divorce, and Remarriage in the Bible* by Jay E. Adams; and *Remarriage and God's Renewing Grace* by Dwight Small.

From my own personal study and experience, I have come to the conclusion that remarriage is possible for a divorced person. However, each situation has its own circumstances and therefore must be viewed, evaluated, and decided on its own merits. God's grace is sufficient to help us learn from our mistakes. We can know forgiveness is available when needed to help us deal with failure in creative ways. However, if a remarriage is to last, it should be grounded in an understanding and acceptance of God's design for marriage: a companionship of the highest degree based in total commitment and loyalty to each other. If children are involved, it should be grounded in an understanding of what a blended family is and how it can best function (a thorough discussion of blended families follows in the next chapter). It should be grounded in the idea that marriage is a partnership, and can function effectively when certain ingredients are a part of that partnership (as mentioned earlier).

Suppose You Don't Marry?

What if the reality of the future, as you now see it, doesn't include the possibility that your long desired dream of marriage will be coming true? Is a new dream possible? How do you change a dream? Is it possible to have a perception of life that affirms that it's okay to married and it's okay to be single?

Part of the concern with some single adults today is a matter of perception. If we perceive the single life-style as a totally negative experience (constant pity-parties, loneliness, weeping, feeling unattractive and unwanted, frightened and desperate), we transfer to others those perceptions in our expression of what it means to be who we are. Our actions usually bare to others these traits and these others validate what they see by either avoidance or just putting up with us. No one likes to be around a negative person. Our actions may lead us to questionable relationships (possible promiscuity), a pulling away, being a total bore, constant bickering, or being just plain mad at the world.

Can we then come to accept our singleness with a perception that says, **It's okay to be single?** I believe it is. Is it possible to change a dream? I believe we can. I also believe it has to start with our acceptance of reality. If you are not now married to someone **You are a single adult**. It may be true that you didn't want to be single but you are. That's reality—and that has to be okay because, although it can be changed, for now it is real. It is who you are. It doesn't presuppose you will remain single for the rest of you life, but for now you are a single adult. We know that as long as we're alive there's always the possibility for a martial relationship to blossom.

So, we can change our dream in part by accepting reality, and we continue to change it by consciously reassuring ourselves that we can be one of the happiest single adults alive. A great many pluses and minuses are related to the single life, just as there are to married life. I can be thankful for the good and minimize the negatives when I "accept the things I cannot change; [asking God to give me the] courage to change the things I can and the wisdom to know the difference."

"What lies behind us and what lies before us are tiny matters compared to what lies within us."*
—Vicki Lansky

The Reality of Single Parenting

Would it not be unbelievably wonderful if, as a single parent with children at home, you had the physical strength and stamina of a superman or superwoman; the emotional stability to "be cool" all the time; grandparents close and eager enough to take the children anytime you wanted; a supportive network of ten or more concerned, listening friends; and a cook and a maid? Wouldn't it be wonderful? Ah, dream on, dream on.

This chapter will deal with issues faced by single parent families, whether they were created by death, divorce, adoption, or mistake. It will attempt to view the issues from the parent's as well as the child's point of view. The organizations listed at the end can be of tremendous help. The books listed in the bibliography are not an extensive list but ones chosen for their clarity and comprehensive comments on the issues involved and positive ways to deal with them.

Definition of a Single Parent

If you've been suddenly made single by divorce or death and you and your former spouse had children and they are living with you, you are a single parent. If you are raising an adopted child or children by yourself, you are a single parent. If you had a child or children and never married and are raising that child by yourself, you are a single parent. If your former spouse has custody of your child or children and you are with your child periodically, you are a single parent. Being one isn't easy, as I'm sure you can attest if you are one.

Certain issues evolve out of certain circumstances. However, all single parents have to deal with raising the children, financial issues, developing a support system, dating, and the possibility of a blended family. Divorced and widowed single parents have to think about the possibility of remarriage—and, specifically, divorced single parents have to work through the ramifications of custody.

Raising the Children

To pinpoint specifics here is difficult because each situation is so different. Children are at various ages, and the parents involved come to the issues differently because of their personal histories. The divorced and widowed experience many kinds of adjustments to the new history about to be lived. Hence, countless books have been written about raising children as a single parent (see the bibliography).

Bobbie Reed, in her book *Single Mothers Raising Sons* suggests four basic responses to the problems and joys of single parenting. Although the book is directed at mothers raising sons, the responses are enough alike for fathers as well to merit our attention. The first response she says is "I can't do anything," meaning "I'm not capable of what this will demand of me." A second type says "I'll do it or die," meaning: "I **must** do everything myself and cannot fail, I'm in control." The third type is "I'm surviving," meaning: "I think I can see some light at the end of the tunnel if I just take it one day at a time." Last, a fourth type says "I'm doing okay," meaning: "I realize nobody's perfect but I'm an important person as well as a parent, and besides, this too shall pass."

This suggests a progression, in a way. In the earlier stages, adjustment seems an overwhelming task, but as we "persevere," we move toward acceptance, just as in other adjustments. The key, I believe, is developing and maintaining a positive self-image and a high level of self-esteem. I also believe that a lot of that comes from a personal relationship with God and with the Bible. I would refer you to chapters four and five for specifics.

Raising children alone is a most challenging job. I know I haven't written in specifics to help with the challenge, but maybe the best we can do is to put a great deal of effort into **raising ourselves**. As we do, we can teach and train, even if we are just one. We **can** set a good example. We **can** help our children be with role models who are healthy and positive. We **can** make discipline work. Even though life has its ups and downs, from experience we know good times will come eventually. We also know that there will be struggles. We **can** also know and believe God can and wants to see us through, providing us the right kind of wisdom and strength.

Financial Issues

Whether you're a single parent or not, money matters are usually always an issue. But single parents have special concerns. Regardless of the reason why one is a single parent, women in general (by far the majority have custody) fear they won't be able to survive financially—and rightly so, given the statistics. On the average, a woman's income decreases by some seventy percent after a divorce. A little over a quarter (twenty-six percent) of divorced mothers **never receive any child support at all.** Though some changes are being made by child-support legislation, it's slow in coming. Another reason for the fear is that they may not have developed skills needed in the work force and even if they have them, they are often paid less than men for them. In divorce and widowhood a significant decline in a familiar standard of living is experienced. In a divorce particularly, child support is usually a bone of contention simply because no two individuals seem able to agree on what is fair or reasonable. Add two lawyers to the mix and you have four opinions.

Winning the Reader's Digest million dollar sweepstake would be most helpful, but you just can't count on it. What you can do, however, is to concentrate on skill development. This may take the form of enrolling in a night course on money management or going back to school for a degree. Naturally, this will be difficult to do with children to care for. Some fortunate single parents have grandparents nearby who have been most helpful with caring for the children when needed. Others have teamed up with other single parents and have worked out mutual care. The aim of skill development is independence. With it you can work toward making it on your own.

Some other possible options include learning how to make and keep a budget. Many books can be found on the subject in the library. One especially helpful to divorced single parents is *Financial Fitness through Divorce* by Elizabeth S. Lewin. Because of the Federal Child Support Enforcement Amendment (1984) you can get employers of your former spouse to withhold child support from his or her wages if the person is thirty days delinquent in their payments.

There is a free booklet about this called *Handbook on Child Support Enforcement* available from Consumer Information Center, Box 100, Dept. CS, Pueblo, CO., 81009.

Developing a Support System

New families require new relationships. Single parents need ties outside their homes. This is particularly true of the single parent who is the head of the household. In marriage the spouse enjoyed some security in knowing that someone was there to help, be available in case of emergencies, assume some of the responsibility. Because that person is no longer available as he or she once was, the single parent needs to work at establishing a network of support.

The more obvious place to go to create this base would be friends, relatives, or friendly neighbors. To be sure in some instances some of these may prove limited in their capability of understanding your situation. But, a parent or brother or sister or neighbor may be just the one for you. If a new set of friends is needed you may find some sympathetic to your plight at a meeting/conference/seminar on single parenting. These are sometimes conducted through your church or local hospital. Friends also come from parents of your children's friends. Remember, however, friendship is a two-way street. You take what you need but you also give what you can.

Might you be the catalyst for starting a support group for single parents? You could suggest, through your church newsletter or other such medium, a luncheon for single parents to discuss the possibilities. At the luncheon you could come prepared to suggest a meeting time and place. You could also suggest possible program ideas, such as a guest speaker, a book to review on single parenting (see bibliography), a "brag night" (sharing accomplishments of your children), development of strategies to assist one another when needed, and the like. Are you the one to get the ball rolling?

Psalm 84, among other passages in the Bible, suggests another support that's available just for the asking. The psalm is a song of celebration sung or chanted by pilgrims on their way to the temple in Jerusalem. They were on the way to the temple to express their thanks for the fall harvest and to praise God for God's constant care. The psalm speaks of valleys the pilgrims would have to go through to get to the temple, dry and barren places. But because of their gladness of heart in wanting to give thanks for God's blessings, the valleys were like "places of springs." Why? They knew how to gain their strength from God. They continued on through the valleys, going from "strength to strength" leaning on God to see them through.

In the book *I Go Horizontal*, Duff Gilford, the author, portrays a vivid picture of what laying for *ten years* in the flat, level world of sleeping sickness was like. The book, at least for some, probably defines a common plight. All too often we find ourselves knocked flat, in dry and barren places, and we get our motives for living from this flat, often material, world. We depend on things, gimmicks, drugs. We fail to realize that there is another way to approach life, that there can be vertical living. We need to accept as fact that we can find support from God. We can establish a relationship with God that can see us through. Another psalm affirms, "I will lift up my eyes to the hills—where does my help come from? My help comes from the Lord, the Maker of heaven and earth" (Psalm 121:1).

Consider the flowers and the sun. If you examine a flower bulb, it comes close to looking like a retired onion. It doesn't look very promising. But expose that bulb to the earth and the warmth and pull of the sun, and something in that flower says, "This is what I was made for," and it rises up and blooms. It was exposed to that which fits its nature. As children of God we've been made to enjoy God's strength. It's not for someone else. It's for everyone who will assume a vertical position. It's for anyone who will look up and see him who was lifted up and said of himself "I will draw all men [and women] unto me." That's good news, and Jesus said it.

God's strength is available to be our support. Jesus assured us before he left this temporal world, "You shall receive power." Through the Holy Spirit, people have found it as he said. The words that early Christians in the first century cried out, "I can do everything through him [meaning Jesus Christ] who gives me strength" (Philippians 4:13) have been repeated down through the centuries and can be repeated by you.

Dating

Single parents are available for new relationships. That means the possibility of dates. For some who haven't been in the "game" for a while, it can be scary. One of the problems that seems to crop up in this area is that a number of your friends think they know someone who is the perfect date for you. You may not be ready, and if that's the way you feel, you need to be honest about it with these people. Married friends, relatives, single friends, and even casual acquaintances feel a sense of obligation to help you meet someone "special." These match-makers mean well but often don't realize the burden of scrutiny that could occur. Because of their involvement, they wonder how the date went and you have to report. You feel you're back in a child-parent relationship. On the other hand, some single parents are fortunate. A new relationship forms in a natural way. You meet someone at a party or at church or while shopping.

You share some common interest and an invitation for further conversation is offered. Then there are other meetings (dates) and a relationship happens, almost effortlessly. For others it's not that simple. Early in the dating game, many feel awkward and ill at ease. Many of these issues have been discussed in chapter eight; however, there are some differences.

With single parents there is the whole issue of conflict of demand. Some single parents, because they are torn between the demands of a new relationship and the needs of their children, hesitate to date. Some children even openly object to their parent's dating because it's another activity taking the parent away from the home. For some children, particularly teen-agers, dating suggests that their parent is a sexual human being. That may be hard for them to understand (think about how you feel about your own parents). Among those who are widowed is the fear that no new relationship can compare with what they once experienced. Those separated or divorced might feel just the opposite. They may feel the fear that a new relationship would be similar to what they just suffered through. These and other issues are at stake and must be worked through. Everyone has her or his own approach to handling these issues. Some sort of support group can be helpful, particularly if you know of others who have already worked through some of these issues and can ask for their advice.

Remarriage

Some statistics say that about ninety percent of those who divorce will remarry. Of those who do, fifty-five to sixty percent will divorce again. Why? Among the reasons are the realization that they didn't give themselves enough time to examine their own motives and the issues involved with blended families. Most authorities would say that those who are divorced or widowed should give themselves at least two years before entering into a new marriage. They should use that time to answer as honestly as possible, Who am I now that I'm no longer in a marriage, and what do I want to do with the rest of my life?

For some, remarriage after divorce is a theological issue. If, for whatever reason, you feel concern at this point, I would highly recommend the following two books: *Remarriage and God's Renewing Grace* by Dwight Hervey Small and *Divorce and Remarriage in the Bible* by Kenneth E. Jones. Both of these books deal with those passages in the Bible related to this whole issue that seem so hard to understand.

Blended Families

Call it what you will, blended family, stepfamily, reconstituted family, or extended family, all of these terms designate a new family formed by a previous marriage. It is not a biological family (couple with their own children). It is born of the loss of a parent from the home and a partner from a relationship, followed by the introduction of a stepparent, a new partner. It requires special understanding and some unique adjustments by both adults and children.

Part of that understanding comes from acknowledging and disbelieving some of the myths that make the process of blending much more difficult. Some of those include the following:

Myth #1-You will experience instant love for your spouse's children. Most would agree that this is the ideal but it doesn't happen (instantly at least). Children serve as a constant reminder of a previous intimate relationship. This brings mixed feelings, even some resentment. These all influence the relationship.

Myth #2-You will love all children equally. This is a biological myth. A relationship has been developed with a natural child over the years. To believe that everyone can instantly love a stepchild with the same intensity one loves a natural child is to deny the biological tie. A genuinely deep affection can develop between a child and stepparent, but it is likely to be different and to require time.

Myth #3-The children must be first. A stepfamily is an "instant" family. There is no "childless" time to build the love bond between the couple. Personalities are already formed. **The effective task of any stepfamily**

depends primarily upon the relationship, both marital and parental, of the stepparenting couple. If this is developing strongly and solidly, the stepfamily has a great chance of meeting adequately the needs of the children.

Myth #4-The stepfamily is a biological family. It just can't be. A stepfamily differs because it has been born of loss. A new person enters an established relationship, but another biological parent is out there (a presence even if dead) that affects new ties, and the adults have at least one marital history from which they must begin to do things differently.

Custody

One of the main issues here is civility. When a couple with children decide to break up the foundation that once represented a traditional family, a partnership is lost. Different incomes, homes, and other people now enter the picture. The couple usually meet only when the parent without custody visits the children, at which time pain games can take place. Using the children as messengers, spies, or as leverage are a few. Children can play, too. They can and do pit one parent against the other to get what they want. Other pain games include the noncustodial parent making plans to be with the children and not showing up; the custodial parent refusing to change plans so the other parent, who has some unexpected time and wants to be with the children, can spend some time with them. These and more cause hurt and anger. When former spouses meet, words elicit gestures and flare into heated arguments. Hence, how can I be civil?

Anger is natural. But one has to come to grips with its effects and how long one is going to let it control the situation. Usually, an unrealistic demand is behind much anger. The demand in most custody situations is that the other parent will stop playing games, put the children first, and treat you like a human being when you have to meet (which you may like to be once a year). If that's your demand, it's unrealistic, and it could be the source of some of your anger. If you can change the demand to a wish, and begin to put the energy you use being angry into learning how to be a better custodial or noncustodial parent, you might move from hostility to civility.

One more comment needs to be made on the other side of the coin. A friendly divorce is a myth. To think that you can be friends when divorced after years of commitment and sharing is unreasonable because it hinders the emotional process that must take place if one is to answer effectively, Who am I now that I'm no longer in a marriage? It's unreasonable because it gets in the way of your effectively quitting your marriage. It's unreasonable because it could be harmful and confusing to the children. (They think,

If you are friendly now, why did you get a divorce?) It's hard because to suppose that two people who couldn't get along when married will do so when they are divorced is unrealistic.

What needs to happen is that as soon as possible the couple needs to concentrate on being civil (kind, decent, honest, and so on) with each other and allow each the freedom to leave the marriage and begin a fresh start. Being civil doesn't imply there is a relationship. It does provide a way to interact with another. True it is not easy, particularly if you're in the early stages of separation and divorce. But it is a direction toward which you can be headed.

A host of other issues could be raised about custody but it seems to me the sooner a father and mother can move toward civility, the better off everyone will be. Other pressing concerns will begin to subside, and adjustment to the transition can take place with some sense of decency.

Where's the Help?

The books listed in the bibliography for this chapter have been selected from a vast number available. I've found them both concise and easy to understand. Others are available at your public library. The following is a list of associations, agencies, and organizations that can be very helpful in supplying up-to-date information about single-parent issues.

The Aring Institute
6881 Beechmont Ave.
Cincinnati, OH 45230
513-231-6630

The Greater Minneapolis Association of
Evangelicals
6108 Excelsior Blvd.
Minneapolis, MN 55416

The Sisterhood of Black Single Mothers, Inc.
1360 Fulton St., Room 433
Brooklyn, NY 11216

The American Institute of Family-Relations
9942 Vineland Ave.
N. Hollywood, CA 91601

North American Council on Adoptable Children, Inc.
3900 Market Street, Suite 247
Riverside, CA 92501

The Stepfamily Association America
602 East Joppa Rd.
Baltimore, MD 21204
301-823-7570

The Stepfamily Foundation
333 West End Ave.
New York, NY 10023
212-877-3244

Parents Without Partners
8807 Colesville Rd.
Silver Spring, MD
301-588-9354

The following agencies can offer information about services available in your area.

Family Service Association of America
44 East 23rd St.
New York, NY 10010

The United Way of America
801 North Fairfax
Alexandria, VA 22314

God desires an intimate relationship with each one of us.

The Reality of God and Growing Spiritually

In relation to the Senate's traditional opening prayer Senator Robert C. Byrd said the following: "It should be kind of sobering to us, as we listen to these prayers every morning, to know that when we have finished our work here, the Senate will go on, the world will go on. They will continue to hold roll-call votes open for Senators who are a little late getting here. The sun will shine, the moon will rise, seasons will come and go, and the only thing that really, really will matter will be the eternal and spiritual side of life."

I believe that and I trust you do, too. I also believe that there are other "sides" of me that compete with the growth and development of this all-important spiritual side. I know, for example, that other parts of myself are a physical side, an emotional or feeling side, an intellectual side, and a social or relational side. Wanting to take care of my physical body seems easy for me (by feeding it nutritious food, providing for adequate sleep, and participating in daily exercise).

To stimulate my mind through reading and discussion also seems easy for me, because of my desire to learn and better myself. Working at relating to other people also seems easy for me because I happen to believe that I need other people reacting to me and my life-style, if I'm to come to some understanding of the meaning of life. However, always to understand or be able to express my feelings or emotions is not easy for me. Yet, I realize that these feelings are very much a part of who I am, and I need to strengthen the positive ones and work at eliminating the negatives. Because all this is going on within me at the same time, to allot the proper time, energy, and effort to nurture and develop my spiritual side is not so easy. I find myself constantly striving for **balance**, which I believe is a key word in this whole area of spiritual growth and development.

Many singles to whom I talk feel some of these same tensions and the pain of the struggle. So, the rest of this chapter will deal with some important questions related to this all-important issue. How do I know I have a spiritual side? How do I nurture and develop it? What gets in the way of its healthy growth? What are the evidences that it's developing in positive ways?

How Do I Know I Have a Spiritual Side?

I asked this question of a Sunday school

152

class of single adults who meet in a restaurant in Anderson, Indiana. Their answers included comments like these: because we have a conscience; because I have experienced definite and real answers to prayer; and, of course, because we have a book (the Bible) that has come down to us through the ages and tells us we have one. Paul, in writing to the Corinthians specifically says we are spiritual: "If there is a physical body, there is also a spiritual body" (1 Corinthians 15:44). The Bible speaks of the "image of God," which is part of all of us since creation. That image speaks to us internally that we are spiritual beings. (For more about the image of God in us see again the discussion in chapter five.)

So, whether I choose to believe it or not, I am a spiritual being. Because I am, I can experience a relationship with God, and that relationship can change my life.

How Do I Nurture and Develop My Spiritual Side?

First, I believe I must recognize that God wants to help me. I'm not alone in the "battle of the balance." I must believe that God is at work in my own personal struggle and experience. Therefore, I have to stay awake and be aware. I need to continue to ask God to teach me, through life's experiences and by his Holy Spirit. I need to be taught who he is and how he relates to me and I to him.

In this recognition I also come to realize that this is a continual process. I can't assume I'll ever know all there is to know about God and God's plan for my life. It will keep evolving as I keep searching. The important point is that I continue to ask to be taught.

Second, I nurture and develop my spiritual side by accepting God's love, mercy, and forgiveness and assume the disciplines that follow that acceptance. Because of my acceptance of these qualities I then can show others love, mercy, and forgiveness. In that process, I find my spiritual side expanding and becoming a vital part of my life-style.

Back in the late seventies Richard Foster wrote *Celebration of Discipline*. In it he gathered together the classical disciplines needed to develop our spiritual side to the fullest. The inward disciplines are meditation, prayer, fasting, and study. The outward disciplines include simplicity, solitude, submission, and service. The corporate disciplines are confession, worship, guidance, and celebration. These are key activities in which to engage if I'm to develop my spiritual side.

Third, I nurture and develop my spiritual side by seeking to be like God as much as is humanly possible. My example here is Jesus Christ. In order for me to get a clear picture of him I have to come to know him as personally as I can. I need to know why he came, what happened to those he touched, and what he taught. One very effective way of finding this precious information is through reading the Bible. I can find some of this in worship and by listening to biblical preaching, but personal study can reveal some treasures that can come to me only because of God's personal contact with me through God's Word and the Holy Spirit's guidance. There are indeed treasures to be found, but I can't find them unless I look.

I'm reminded of a story I heard about a somewhat spoiled boy who graduated from high school and was hoping to get a car to take with him to college. But it didn't happen. Instead his dad gave him a Bible and told him to read it, suggesting that he would find treasures for living in its pages. The boy went off to college disappointed. He came home after his first year, now thinking he would get his long-awaited car. But his father asked him if he had read the Bible he had given him. The boy said he had looked at it. His dad told him he couldn't have the car yet. This went on throughout the next three years and each year the boy was disappointed because his dad wouldn't give him a car. Each year the boy went back to college promising to read the Bible. Finally, graduation day arrived. Surely, the boy thought, now his dad would give him a car. But it didn't happen. His dad came to the graduation ceremonies without any keys but with the same question: Did you read the Bible I gave you? The boy answered, "Well, I looked at it."

"Well son, if you would have opened its pages and read it you would have found a check for fifteen thousand dollars in it for your new car."

Last, I nurture and develop my spiritual side by doing something specific about my faith. Paul told the Corinthians that he was a servant of Christ. As I develop my spiritual side, I need to respond by discovering what being a "servant of Christ" means. How have I, for example, accepted the challenge to be a disciple of Christ? In what ways am I seriously seeking to know God's will as I relate to the needs around me? One very helpful book related to effective servanthood is Charles Swindoll's *Improving Your Serve*. The book is tremendously beneficial in defining the portrait of one who serves. It also provides insight into a servant's influences, hazards, consequences, and rewards. The servant life is an unselfish life that can be learned. It doesn't take great wisdom; just a willing spirit that says, "Show me, Lord."

In Galatians we find that Christ has freed us to "serve one another in love" (Galatians 5:13). When we find ourselves serving others in love we are developing and nurturing our spiritual side.

What Gets in the Way of Healthy Growth?

Probably, one of the major attitudes that prevents us from healthy spiritual growth is our inability to accept the challenge of balance. As mentioned earlier, if I don't set aside some priority time to work actively at this important part of my development as a human being, it won't get done. No one can set the time or place but me. No one can tell me what I need to do but me. No one can tell me what God wants me to do but God. It's my responsibility, if I choose to accept it, to make balance happen. I can ignore or deny that I really need to work at this. I can also deny I even need God but if I do I'm the loser, no one else.

Another deterrent to healthy spiritual growth involves centering our thoughts and observations on the shortcomings of "religious" people. People can easily point a finger and say, "If that's Christianity, I don't want any part of it." They may experience difficulty in realizing that people are human beings, and, try as they may, experience difficultly in always being who we feel they ought to be. I'm not excusing blatant sinful behavior. Sin is sin. It separates us from God. However, there is mercy and forgiveness and the privilege of new beginnings. Someone said it well, "Human beings are clay pots, not finished porcelain." If you want someone to look at for an example, examine the life and teachings of Jesus Christ. He won't disappoint you.

Another hindrance to healthy spiritual growth is self-centeredness—the attitude that puts "me-ism" front and center. This usually expresses itself in totally selfish living. It's the "What's in it for me?" attitude.

One is so preoccupied with looking out for number one that all energy and time is consumed with satisfying either physical, emotional, or relational needs. These simply crowd out time for spiritual growth.

Last, (but by no means have we exhausted the list), we hinder our spiritual growth when we are unable to trust the Bible as God's Word. If we believe the Bible to be simply another book with some neat stories in it, we can't expect it to have any influence on our life other than to entertain us. If, however, by faith we are able to effect within ourselves an assured attitude toward the Bible (which may rest on evidence of experience, knowledge, respect, and reverence) and its promises, we can expect it to make a difference and have lasting value. It is the one book that speaks specifically and effectively to our spiritual development.

Evidences of Positive Growth

One of the first evidences of spiritual development is that I experience a certain peace of mind about it. If I'm working at it, I don't have to feel guilty. So, the absence of guilt helps my peace of mind. This peace of mind is also part of the peace promised by God. Jesus Christ promised the disciples (then and now) "another counselor . . . , the Spirit of truth" who would teach us all things. He then reminds them (and us) of a blessing he wished to bestow on them (and us).

"Peace I leave with you; my peace I give you" (John 14:27). As I develop my spiritual side I begin to discover what I need to accept and to claim the promises of God, one of which is God's peace.

As I develop my spiritual side, God becomes real to me. In the process I am becoming more aware that I need God in my life. I can, if I choose, muster up all the determination and courage humanly possible to live out the life God has called me to live. But I soon realize I just can't do it by myself. I'm called to reflect God's character in my life, to reflect righteousness, love, justice, and mercy in all that I do, think, feel, and say. But because I am very much a human being, prone to doing just the opposite, I find I am not like God. I need God in my life. As I acknowledge this, God becomes real to me.

I think this is beautifully illustrated in the delightful story told by Bob Benson in his book *See You at the House*. It's about a Sunday school picnic to which you want to go but discover that all you find to take is a stale baloney sandwich. So, you take it because you want to be with friends. When the time to eat comes, you sit at the end of a table, kind of sheepishly embarrassed, and spread out your sandwich. Some people sit down next to you and begin to lay out a tremendous spread of fried chicken, baked beans, potato salad, homemade rolls, pickles, olives, and two big homemade chocolate pies. They say to you, "Why don't we put it all together?" "No," you say, "I couldn't do that." But they insist, "Oh, come on, there's plenty of everything and we just love baloney sandwiches. Let's just put it all together." And so you do and there you sit eating like a king when you came like a pauper.

Bob concludes with this thought. "And I get to thinking—I think of me 'sharing' with God. When I think of how little I bring, and how much he brings and that he invites me to 'share,' I know I should be shouting to the housetops, but I am so filled with awe and wonder that I can hardly be heard. . . . It's not that he needs your sandwich—the fact is, you need his chicken."

Another evidence has to do with the Bible itself. It is slowly but surely moving from the coffee table (or wherever it's been kept) into the study and into one's life and actions. The "book" is becoming more then a book. Its "ring of truth" is beginning to resonate deep within. As I devote more time to its pages I learn more and more about this mysterious and available God who fills up its pages. I am beginning to learn about its promises and beginning to realize they are mine to believe and have faith in and to appropriate into my life.

Last (though again by no means have we exhausted this list either), as I develop my spiritual side, I find I'm a little more capable of coping with life's ups and downs with a little more assurance. The idea that I'm not alone in this project of making the most out of my life is beginning to sink in. I'm in a partnership with God. As a result I have available to me someone who knows all about the territory and is willing and able, when necessary, to carry me through the valleys and up to the top of the hills.

There's a delightfully encouraging poem that suggests the importance of God's part· nership. It's called "Footprints" (author unknown). It speaks of the complaint of a man who, looking back at his life through a dream, remembers two sets of footprints symbolizing what he believed to be his own and God's as he moved through life. But when the man went through hard times, low times, there was only one set of footprints and the man believed them to be his own. He also believed that at those times God had left him to work out his own problems. Hence, his complaint. But the dream concludes with God saying to him, "My precious, precious child, I love you and I would never, never leave you. During your times of trial and suffering when you saw only one set of footprints—that was when I carried you."

Conclusion

Our calling to develop our spiritual side is not to remove ourselves from ordinary life or to deprive ourselves of our personality or to divide life up into two neat segments— life here (physical, human, secular, and so forth) and life "up there" (spiritual, supernatural, sacred). Our calling involves us in believing and acting out the spiritual truth: we have been created to love God and enjoy God forever. Our calling invites us to reflect God's character in all of life, here and now. Our calling is not to be replaced by the Spirit, but it is to be constantly flavored by asking the Holy Spirit to help us be restored to the image of God, God's likeness. In that way we can adequately reflect God's righteousness, love, justice, and mercy. We effectively develop our spiritual side by loving God and allowing God's Holy Spirit to help us become like him. The way is one of becoming.

Let the following words written as a paraphrase of part of Philippians 3 by Leslie Brandt be your personal "manifesto" as you strive to develop effectively your spiritual side and face the reality and beauty of living life to its fullest as a single adult.

Jesus Christ is sufficient and so is the righteousness that He imparts to us. We don't earn or merit or gain it by following certain rules or rituals; we receive it as the gift of God's love. We possess this righteousness even now by faith in Christ. We have no need for any other. This by no means indicates that we have arrived—that we have already reached the ultimate in our natural state of being. We do, indeed, belong to God; we are His possession. And yet we struggle constantly to surrender our total beings to Him—to let Him have His way with us. This does not come easily. It involves the crucible of conflict—even failure and defeat. But even when we fall, we fall only to rise again. Acknowledging but never nursing our failures, we claim God's gracious forgiveness and carry on, knowing that our loving God understands and perpetually reaches out to draw us to Himself. Even while we are God's sons and daughters, **we are in the process of becoming**. Our creation is not yet completed and won't be until we break through this mortal shell to become perfectly and eternally united to God. Meanwhile our citizenship is in God's kingdom, and we are here to advance that kingdom throughout our sorry world (*Epistles Now* by Leslie Brandt, page 103).

Bibliograghy

Chapter 1—The Reality of Being Single

Edwards, Marie and Eleanor Hoover. *The Challenge of Being Single*. New York: Signet, 1974.

Hadidan, Allen. *A Single Thought; God's Thought on Singleness*. Chicago: Moody Press, 1981.

Harbour, Brian L. *Famous Singles of the Bible*. Nashville: Broadman, 1980.

Karssen, Glen. *Getting the Most Out of Being Single*. Colorado Springs: NavPress, 1982.

Meredith, Don. *Who Says Get Married?*. Nashville: Thomas Nelson, 1981.

Reed, Bobbie. *Making The Most of Single Life*. St. Louis: Concordia Publishing House, 1980.

Smith, Harold Ivan. *Positively Single*. Wheaton, IL: Victor Books, 1986.

Yoder, Bruce and Ima Jeanne, eds. *Single Voices*. Scotsdale, PA: Herald Press, 1982.

Chapter 2—The Reality of Freedom

Adler, Mortimer. *Ten Philosophical Mistakes*. New York: McMillian, 1985.

Barnette, Henlee. *Your Freedom to Be Whole*. Philadelphia: Westminster Press, 1984.

Fagerstrom, Douglas L, ed. Chapter 23, "Sexuality and Moral Choices." *Singles Ministry Handbook*. Wheaton, IL: Victor Books, 1988.

Nelson, Richard C. *Choosing to be Whole*. Philadelphia: Westminster Press, 1984.

Rubin, Theodore Isaac. *Overcoming Indecisivness*. New York: Harper & Row, 1985.

Chapter 3—The Reality of Wholeness

Adams, Jay E. *A Thirst for Wholeness*. Wheaton, IL: SP Publications, 1988.

Anderson, Ann Kiemel and Jan Kiemel Ream. *Struggling for Wholeness*. Nashville, TN: Nelson, 1986.

Barnette, Henlee. *Your Freedom to Be Whole*. Philadelphia: The Westminster Press, 1984.

Collins, Gary. *Calm Down*. Ventura, CA: Vision House, 1981.

Cooper, Kenneth. *The Aerobics Program for Total Wellbeing*. New York: M. Evans, 1982.

Dobson, James. *Emotions: Can You Trust Them?* Ventura, CA: Vision House, 1981.

Hazelip, Harold. *Lord, Help Me When I'm Hurting*. Grand Rapids, MI: Baker Book House, 1984.

O'Connor, Elizabeth. *Our Many Selves*. New York: Harper & Row, 1971.

Paul, Cecil and Jan Lanham. *Choices: In Pursuit of Wholeness*. Kansas City, MO: Beacon Hill Press, 1982.

Salter, Debbie. *One Is More Than un*. Kansas City, MO: Beacon Hill Press, 1978.

Wackman, Daniel, Elam Nunnally, Sherod Miller. *Alive and Aware?* Minneapolis, MN: Interpersonal Communications Programs, 1976.

Chapter 4 & 5—The Reality of Self-Esteem Parts 1 and 2

CA Task Force to Promote Self-Esteem. Sacramento, CA.

Glasser, William. *Positive Addiction*. New York: Harper & Row, 1976.

Newman, Mildred and Bernard Berkowitz. *How to Be Your Own Best Friend*. Center City, MN: Hazelden, 1984.

Seamands, David A. Chapter 10, "Grace and Self-Esteem," *Healing Grace*. Wheaton, IL: Victor Books, 1988.

Simon, Sidney. *I Am Loveable and Capable*. Niles, IL: Argus Communications, 1973.

Chapter 6—The Reality of Loneliness and Solitude

Briggs, Dorothy. *Celebrate Yourself*. New York: Doubleday, 1977.

Byrd, Richard E. *Alone*. New York: G. P. Putnam's Sons, 1938.

Merton, Thomas. *Thoughts in Solitude*. New York: Farrar, Straus & Giroux, 1976.

Moustakas, Clark E. *Loneliness*. Englewood Cliffs, NJ: Prentice-Hall, 1961.

Morris, Peter. *Loss and Change*. New York: Doubleday & Co., 1975.

Neale, Robert. *Loneliness, Solitude, & Companionship*. Philadelphia: Westminster Press, 1984.

Riesman, David, ed. *The Lonely Crowd*. New York: Yale University Press, 1973.

Sarton, May. *Journal of a Solitude*. New York: W.W. Norton, 1977.

Weiss, Robert. *Loneliness: The Experience of Emotional and Social Isolation*. Cambridge, MA: MIT Press, 1974.

Chapter 7—The Reality of Friendship
Buscaglia, Leo. *Loving Each Other*. New Jersey: Slack Incorporated, 1984.

Engstrom, Ted. *The Fine Art of Friendship*. New York: Thomas Nelson, 1985.

Inrig, Gary. *Quality Friendship*. Chicago: Moody Press, 1981.

Neale, Robert. *Loneliness, Solitude, and Companionship*. Philadelphia, PA: Westminster Press, 1984.

Zimbardo, Philip. *Shyness: What It Is, What to Do About It*. Reading, MA: Addison-Wesley, 1977.

———. *The Shy Child*. New York: McGraw-Hill, 1981.

Chapter 8—The Reality of Dating
Gordon, Sol. *The Teenage Survival Book*. New York: Time Books, 1975.

Parriott, Sara. Futile: *The Magazine of Adult Dating*. New York: Workman Publishing, 1983.

Purnell, Dick. *Becoming a Friend and Lover*. San Bernardino, CA: Here's Life Publishers, 1983.

Wagenwood, James. *Personal Style: The Man's Guide to Fashion, Fitness, Travel, and Entertaining*. New York: Holt, Rinehart & Winston, 1985.

Chapter 9—The Reality of Intimacy

Colman, Barry, ed. *Sex and the Single Christian*. Ventura, CA: Regal Books, 1985.

Cosby, Michael R. *Sex in the Bible*. Englewood Cliffs, NJ: Prentice-Hall, 1984.

Fagerstrom, Douglas L., (ed.). *Singles Ministry Handbook*. Wheaton, IL: Victor Books, 1988

Foster, Richard J. *Money, Sex and Power*. San Francisco, CA: Harper & Row, 1985.

Goergen, Donald. *The Sexual Celibate*. New York: Doubleday, 1979.

Greeley, Andrew M. *Sexual Intimacy*. New York: Seabury Press, 1973.

Hybels, Bill. *Christians in a Sex-Crazed Culture*. Wheaton, IL: SP Publications, 1989.

Miller, Keith and Andrea Wells Miller. *The Single Experience*. Waco, TX: Word Books, 1981.

Purnell, Dick. *Becoming a Friend and Lover*. San Bernardino, CA: Here's Life Publishers, 1986.

Smith, Harold Ivan. *A Part of Me Is Missing*. Irvine, CA: Harvest House Publishers, 1978.

Stafford, Tim. *The Sexual Christian*. Wheaton, IL: Victor Books, 1988.

White, Mel. *Lust, The Other Side of Love*. Old Tappan, NJ: Fleming Revell, 1978.

Chapter 10—The Reality of Break-ups

Colgrove, Melba, Harold Bloomfield, and Peter Williams. *How to Survive the Loss of a Love*. New York: Bantam Books, 1976.

Phillips, Debora and Robert Judd. *How to Fall Out of Love*. New York: Warner Books, Inc. 1982.

Chapter 11—The Reality of a Future Marriage

Adams, Jay E. *Marriage, Divorce, and Remarriage in the Bible*. Grand Rapids, MI: Baker Book House, 1980.

Beattie, Melody. *Beyond Codependency and Getting Better All the Time*. New York: Harper & Row, 1989.

Brown, Bob W. *Getting Married Again*. Waco, TX: Word Incorporated, 1979.

Ellisen, Stanley A. *Divorce and Remarriage in the Church*. Grand Rapids, MI: Zondervan Publishing House, 1977.

Fisher, Roger and William Ury. *Getting to Yes*. New York: Penguin Books, 1983.

Hocking, David. *Marrying Again*. Old Tappan, NJ: Fleming Revell, 1983.

Hosier, Helen. *To Love Again*. Nashville, TN: Abingdon Press, 1985.

Jones, Kenneth E. *Divorce and Remarriage in the Bible*. Anderson, IN: Warner Press, 1989.

Plekker, Robert J. *Divorce and the Christian*. Wheaton, IL: Tyndale House, 1980.

Richards, Larry. *Remarriage: A Healing Gift from God*. Waco, TX: Word, Inc. 1981.

Small Dwight Hervey. *The Right to Remarry*. Old Tappan, NJ: Fleming Revell, 1977.

_____. *Remarriage and God's Renewing Grace*. Grand Rapids, MI: Baker Books, 1986.

Smith, Harold Ivan. *More Than "I Do": An Engaged Couple's Premarital Handbook*. Kansas City, MO: Beacon Hill Press, 1983.

_____. *More Than "I Do": Devotions for the Engaged Couple*. Kansas City, MO: Beacon Hill Press, 1983.

Steele, Paul E. and Charles C. Ryrie. *Meant to Last*. Wheaton, IL: Victor Books, 1983.

Chapter 12—The Reality of Single Parenting

Arent, Ruth P. *Stress and Your Child*. Englewoods Cliff, NJ: Prentice-Hall, Inc. 1984.

Bustanoby, Andre. *Being a Single Parent*. Grand Rapids, MI: Zondervan Publishing House, 1985.

Dinkmeyer, Don, Gary McKay, and Joyce McKay. *New Beginnings*. Champaign, IL: Research Press, 1987.

Gardner, Richard. *The Boys and Girls Book about Divorce*. New York: Jason Aronson Pub., 1970.

_____. *The Boys and Girls Book about Stepfamilies*. New York: Bantam Books, 1972.

_____. *The Parents' Book about Divorce*. New York: Doubleday and Company, 1977.

Hart, Archibald D. *Children and Divorce*. Waco, TX: Word Books, 1982.

Lansky, Vicki. *Divorce Book for Parents*. New York: New American Library, 1989.

Lewin, Elizabeth S. *Financial Fitness Through Divorce*. New York: Fact on File Publication, 1987.

Neiss, Robert. *Going It Alone*. New York: Basic Books, Inc. 1979.

Reed, Bobbie. *I Didn't Plan to Be a Single Parent*. St. Louis: Concordia Publishing House, 1981.

_____. *Single Mothers Raising Sons*. Nashville, TN: Thomas Nelson Publishers, 1988.

Small Dwight Hervey. *Remarriage and God's Renewing Grace*. Grand Rapids, MI: Baker Book House, 1986.

Somerville, Charles and Herman Colomb. *Stepfathers: Struggles and Solutions*. Philadelphia, PA: Westminister Press, 1988.

Walker, Glyniss. *Second Wife, Second Best?*: New York: Doubleday and Company, 1984

Chapter 13—The Reality of Growing Spiritually

Benson, Bob. *See You at the House*. Nashville, TN: Thomas Nelson, 1989.

Brandt, Leslie. *Epistles Now*. St. Louis: Concordia Publishing House, 1974.

Foster, Richard. *Celebration of Discipline*. New York: Harper and Row, 1978.

Swindoll, Charles. *Improving Your Serve*. Waco, TX: Word, Inc., 1981.

Chapter Quotes

Chapter 2

Quote from *Living Quotations for Christians* by Sherwood Eliot Wirt and Kersten Beckstrom (NY: Harper & Row, 1974).

Chapter 3

Quote from an interview with Ann Keimel Anderson and Jan Ream by Rebecca Parat entitled "Our Search for Acceptance" in *Christian Life* magazine, March 1986.

Chapter 5

Quote from *Living Quotations for Christians* by Sherwood Eliot Wirt and Kersten Beckstrom (NY: Harper & Row, 1974).

Chapter 6

From *Quotable Quotations* by Lloyd Cory (Wheaton, IL: Victor Books, 1985).

Chapter 12

Quote from *Divorce Book for Parents* by Vicki Lansky (NY: New American Library, 1989).